# Don't
# Quit Sugar

# Don't Quit Sugar

## WHY SUGARS ARE IMPORTANT FOR YOUR HEALTH

## CASSIE PLATT

hachette
AUSTRALIA

# hachette
## AUSTRALIA

Published in Australia and New Zealand in 2013
by Hachette Australia
(an imprint of Hachette Australia Pty Limited)
Level 17, 207 Kent Street, Sydney NSW 2000
www.hachette.com.au

10 9 8 7 6 5 4 3 2 1

National Library of Australia
Cataloguing-in-Publication data:

Platt, Cassie.
Don't quit sugar / Cassie Platt.

978 0 7336 3209 9 (paperback)

Sugars in human nutrition.
Sugar in the body.
Sugar – Health aspects.
Food habits.
Nutrition.

641.336

Cover and internal design by Seymour Designs
Cover photograph courtesy Getty Images
Author photograph by Nigel Lough
Internal photographs by Cassie Platt
Internal stock photographs courtesy iStockphoto
Typeset in 10/14 Trade Gothic Light
Printed in China by Toppan Leefung Printing Limited

Hachette Australia's policy is to use papers that are natural, renewable and recyclable products and made from wood grown in sustainable forests. The logging and manufacturing processes are expected to conform to the environmental regulations of the country of origin.

# Contents

Introduction 7

1. The Dangers of Quitting Sugar 9

2. Sugar Myths and Truths:
Sorting Fact from Fiction 15

3. Your How-to Guide to Sugar 25

RECIPES 47
Breakfast 51
Light Meals 73
Mains 95
Desserts 117
Extras 139

Further Reading 150
Index 153

# Introduction

There's no questioning the benefit of switching from a junk-food-based diet to a diet based on whole foods. It's when whole-food-centric diets become overly restrictive that problems can occur. Such is the case with sugar.

To my knowledge, there are very few resources which provide an accessible and evidence-based counterargument to sugar restriction. In creating *Don't Quit Sugar*, I hope to fill this gap.

My own understanding of sugar's role in the body has been cultivated through personal experience and extensive research. **Three years ago, I quit sugar, watched my body slowly deteriorate, and then had to claw my way back to health.**

As a nutritionist (and veritable science nerd), I turned my back on every circulating diet fad (Paleo, Primal, vegan, raw vegan, macrobiotic …) and instead began studying the body. I developed a knowledge base centred on human *physiology* – that is, how the body functions as a system of systems – from the cell level up.

Eating habits should *never* be underpinned by ideas of exclusion – it is this mindset that invariably leads to strife. Rather, our food choices should be based on biological and metabolic needs. What we eat should fuel our cells, facilitate growth, repair and reproduction, and, foremost, enable the body to function optimally and asymptomatically at every level.

Sugar is our cells' preferred source of energy and is absolutely critical to proper metabolic function. Eliminating it from the diet is counterintuitive and a direct contravention of the body's basic requirements.

This doesn't green-light soft-drink consumption or a daily candy fix. It simply means that natural sources of sugar – fruit, honey, sweet root vegetables – *need* to be incorporated into the diet, and often. Unfortunately, fearmongering and a slew of media-endorsed anti-sugar rhetoric have – for many – cultivated an all-or-nothing outlook which is misguided and unnecessary.

This book kicks off by highlighting the **very real and serious dangers of sugar restriction**. In most people, elevated adrenal activity wreaks havoc on the thyroid and progressively lowers metabolism (often while you're losing weight and feeling invincible). Chronic coldness, poor digestion, reduced sex drive, hair loss, hormonal imbalances and a slew of other symptoms are telling signs that should never be ignored.

In the second chapter (page 15), I delve into (and debunk) the major **anti-sugar myths**. Sugar alone *does not* cause obesity. Fructose *is not* the dietary evil of all evils. The stark reality is that the science from which these claims stem is often flawed and never definitive. Purified sugars administered alone and in unrealistically large doses behave entirely differently to natural sugars eaten in the context of a balanced diet.

Chapter 3 is your **how-to guide to sugar** (page 25). Here, I explain which sugars are preferable on the basis of how they affect the body – fruit versus starch, fructose versus glucose. You'll learn how to use these sugars (in combination with proteins and fats) to balance blood sugar, reduce stress and maximise energy production.

Finally, I give you my tried-and-tested **recipes** (page 47) and a 7-day meal planner to help you get started (page 148).

Through mindfully incorporating sugar into your diet, it's possible to optimise metabolism and to build *real* and *lasting* whole body health, beginning at the cellular level.

So, whether you've previously quit sugar, or are simply looking for a way to eat healthily and *inclusively* of all the macronutrients, I hope *Don't Quit Sugar* serves you well.

CASSIE

# 1. The Dangers of Quitting Sugar

The body is made up of tens of trillions of cells. Cells form tissues; tissues form organs; and organs make up the body.

Just as solid bricks build a sturdy house, so do optimally functioning cells build a resilient body. Therefore, we want our cells to be operating as efficiently and as effortlessly as possible.

One of the cells' most basic and important functions is energy production. Every minute of every day, cells must convert nutrients from the foods we eat into usable energy to power growth, repair, reproduction and movement.

Sugar – in the form of glucose – will always be the preferred and most efficient fuel source.

When cells are deprived of this go-to fuel, they need to find other ways to become energised. Proteins and fats can both be used to produce energy, but the process is three times as work-intensive – it's inefficient, wasteful, and ultimately a stress on the cells.

*'Quitting sugar' can in this way be hazardous to cell health, with a follow-on effect to other body systems.*

Currently fashionable low- or no-sugar diets spotlight proteins, fats and green vegetables as the most preferable food choices. Fat, in particular, is emphasised as a 'sugar replacement', used to satisfy lingering hunger and tame sugar cravings. Simple sugars are eliminated and starches are discouraged or eaten minimally. The premise is of moving away from a 'sugar metabolism' and instead towards a 'fat metabolism' – that is, forcing the cells to burn fat for energy.

Many people experience profound results through quitting sugar, particularly in the short term. Mentally, there's increased energy, blunted appetite and noticeable mood enhancement. Physically, there's seemingly effortless weight loss.

What most fail to realise is that such changes are attributable to a state of cellular stress and a consequent rise in stress hormones. For three months, six months, perhaps a year (this is affectionately termed the 'honeymoon phase'), stress hormones can make you feel excellent, promoting euphoria and a heightened sense of wellbeing.

But beneath the surface, stress hormones do exactly as their name suggests – they're a stress on the body in its entirety. Prolonged elevation can break down body tissue, impair thyroid function, damage the metabolism and devastate the body physiologically.

## A GUIDE TO THE STRESS RESPONSE

When we don't eat sugar, the body needs to find alternative fuel sources to provide our cells with energy. It does this via two processes:

1. **Lipolysis**, fat breakdown (*lip* – lipid [fat]; *olysis* – breakdown).
2. **Gluconeogenesis**, protein breakdown to create sugar (*gluco* – glucose [sugar]; *neo* – new; *genesis* – creation).

First, the adrenal glands release **adrenaline** to seek out any stored sugar (glycogen) in the liver. On a low- or no-sugar diet, glycogen stores will be empty. So, adrenaline will instead signal for the release of stored body fat to be used as fuel. This is **lipolysis**, the breaking down of fat for energy.

At the same time as adrenaline mobilises fat, the adrenal glands release **cortisol** to break down body tissue. Skeletal muscle, skin tissue and the thymus gland are broken into proteins, which the liver then converts to glucose to raise blood sugar. This is **gluconeogenesis**; by restricting sugar intake, we force the body to create sugar from its own structure.

*Fat loss on a low-sugar diet is largely due to the action of adrenaline, while better moods and increased mental clarity can each be ascribed to high cortisol.*

Adrenaline and cortisol are the **fight or flight stress hormones**, part of the body's **stress response system**. They should be activated only in emergency or real starvation situations when blood sugar is low and food is unavailable.

But, in quitting sugar and depriving our cells of glucose, we mimic real starvation. Adrenaline and cortisol become activated 24/7, working around the clock to provide our cells with energy.

The greater a role these stress hormones play in our daily function, the more stressed our body becomes. Makes sense, right? So, what are the consequences?

*Adrenaline and cortisol: emergencies – lifesaving; chronic – life-taking.*

## DAMAGED METABOLISM

A chronically stressed body prioritises surviving over thriving. Stored fat and tissues represent finite sources of energy. The body knows this. So, it lowers metabolism in order to halt the rate at which it consumes itself.

The **thyroid gland** is the key player here. It controls the body's rate of metabolism by producing the **thyroid hormones T3 and T4**.

**High T3 levels** are associated with an **optimal, fast metabolism**; **low T3 levels** are associated with a **slow metabolism**.

**Quitting sugar will lower T3** in two ways:

1. The thyroid hormones are antagonised by the stress hormones. As adrenaline and cortisol increase, thyroid hormone production decreases.
2. The thyroid only produces T3 in minimal amounts. The majority of T3 is derived from T4, which is converted to T3 in the liver. But this conversion will only happen if the liver is full of glycogen. And glycogen storage requires sufficient dietary glucose.

What's alarming is that thyroid hormone suppression tends to be self-perpetuating. As we lower our metabolism, the liver loses its ability to store sugar. So, even if we do add sugar back into the diet, glycogen will be inadequate and inhibit T4-to-T3 conversion. The body's stressed state

Don't Quit Sugar

will prevail, and with it a lowered metabolism. This can take months or years to undo.

Quitting sugar is *not* the key to long-term metabolic health.

*Body temperature tends to drop when stress hormones are high and T3 levels are low (cold hands, feet and nose are immediate indicators).*

## WEAKENED DIGESTION

As metabolism falls, the passage of food through the digestive tract becomes increasingly slow.

FACT: For the mammal with the lowest metabolic rate – the sloth – digestion of a single meal can take upwards of a week!

On a low- or no-sugar diet, slow digestion is magnified by the actions of the stress hormones. Adrenaline and cortisol prepare the body for emergency 'fight or flight'. This shifts blood flow to the muscles and brain and away from the digestive system.

Continually high stress hormones (as a result of quitting sugar) will block blood flow to the intestinal tract.

De-energised intestines present several problems:

❖ Digestion and assimilation of food is less efficient, leading to nutrient deficiencies.
❖ Barrier function becomes compromised, enabling toxins and undigested food to enter the bloodstream.
❖ Bacterial overgrowth is more likely due to increased transit time (the time taken until food is finally excreted from the body).

Physically, this will present as constipation, gas, bloating or loose stools. Fun times!

## DECREASED IMMUNITY

High levels of stress hormones, lowered metabolism and weakened digestion all synergise to decrease immunity.

If toxins and undigested food are able to cross the intestinal wall into the bloodstream, they can activate the immune response. This has been linked to most autoimmune conditions: allergies, food sensitivities, irritable bowel syndrome, Crohn's disease, asthma, lupus, chronic fatigue syndrome … the list goes on.

Toxins in the blood will overburden the liver and impair detoxification. As a result, the body will be less able to handle exposure to everyday environmental toxins and chemicals. This leads to increased chemical sensitivities.

The stress hormones alone will also suppress immune function.

Remember that cortisol breaks down body tissue to produce sugar. This includes the tissue of the **thymus gland**, a vital component of the immune system. (For those who've never heard of the thymus, it's a small, lobe-shaped organ located just in front of the heart.) A worn-down thymus means impaired immune function.

FACT: The thymus is most active during infancy and pre-adolescence. Childhood body stress (including sugar restriction) can therefore be destructive to immune development.

## SEXUAL AND REPRODUCTIVE ISSUES

This is one to get your attention.

With a low metabolism and high stress hormone activity, the body's production of pro–sex drive hormones (testosterone in men and progesterone in women) slowly dissipates.

Think about it: if fuel is scarce (low metabolism) and the body is working to conserve as much energy as possible, it certainly doesn't want to waste that energy on sex.

Similarly, if stress hormones are high and the body is geared for an emergency, reproduction is pretty low on its list of priorities. Blood flow is shifted to the brain and muscles (fight or flight), making it exceedingly difficult to 'rev up' our sexual organs.

For men, this means impaired sexual performance.

For women, the issue runs a bit deeper. Progesterone – *pro-gestation* – is also the pro-pregnancy hormone. Progesterone falls with a slowing metabolism because the body simply won't cope with the high energy demands of pregnancy. It's an inbuilt protective mechanism.

Low progesterone means imbalanced hormones. Most significantly, oestrogen becomes too high relative to progesterone. And excess oestrogen carries with it a host of negatives. These include accelerated ageing, water retention, immune-system suppression and increased tissue permeability (leaky gut, food allergies and autoimmune conditions).

In the liver, oestrogen accumulates and isn't detoxified. This promotes inflammation, further blocks thyroid function, down regulates metabolism (again!) and perpetuates the body's state of stress. As a result, progesterone fizzles out even more. It's a vicious, vicious cycle.

The take-home message?

For both sexes, quitting sugar can ultimately spell disaster for reproductive function and sexual appetite.

## IMPAIRED GLUCOSE METABOLISM

Ironically, quitting sugar can damage the body's ability to handle sugar.

With minimal or no sugar in the diet, blood sugar levels are chronically low. As a result, the stress hormones crank into high gear to drive blood sugar up (remember: cortisol converts protein to sugar).

At the same time, the reliance on fat for energy increases the cells' exposure to polyunsaturated fatty acids (PUFA). PUFA in the body are toxic and highly susceptible to oxidation. In the cells, they can cause irreparable damage and impair the ability to use sugar as fuel (fats essentially block sugar from getting into the cells).

Sugar – whether eaten or derived from cortisol's breakdown of protein – will consequently remain in the blood, causing high blood sugar. This is a large factor in the development of what we know as insulin resistance, and – later – Type 2 diabetes.

PUFA have also been found to damage the beta cells of the pancreas, which modulate insulin secretion. Damaged beta cells will impair insulin function, again leading to Type 2 diabetes.

This merely scratches the surface of what is certainly a complex and controversial topic. We'll dig deeper in the following chapter.

For now, just recognise that high stress and using fat for fuel each have some seriously negative effects on the body's ability to deal with sugar.

Don't Quit Sugar

## SLEEP ISSUES

The key to quality sleep is optimal energy metabolism.

Every person experiences a drop in blood sugar during the night-time 'fast' (sleeping hours). In healthy sugar-eaters, sugar stored in the liver will be mobilised to raise blood sugar and provide energy until breakfast is eaten. This should occur without any sleep disruption.

When there is no stored sugar in the liver and metabolism is low, elevated stress hormones (particularly adrenaline) will instead provoke a variety of night-time symptoms:

- ❖ insomnia
- ❖ waking with a rapid heart rate
- ❖ difficulty falling asleep or difficulty getting back to sleep if awoken
- ❖ snoring and sleep apnoea
- ❖ nightmares
- ❖ waking during the night to urinate
- ❖ night sweats.

Urination and sweating each involve water excretion. This is a sign of low blood sugar – the body 'dumps' excess water in order to increase sugar concentrations.

It is only through lowering the stress hormones, optimising metabolism and reteaching the liver to store sugar that restful sleep may be restored.

## ACCELERATED AGEING

One of the main differences between youth and old age is that the elderly burn more fat and less glucose as their primary source of energy. **Fat metabolism is a hallmark of ageing**.

This exposes the cells to toxic PUFA, which are known to cause age-related tissue damage. On the skin, tissue damage manifests as age spots, and often reflects similar degradation occurring inside the body.

Ageing is also associated with a low metabolism, which impairs the body's ability to remove inactive cells and cellular debris. If cellular debris is not removed, regeneration and healing cannot take place. Ageing can in this way be seen as a progressive failure to regenerate.

Why, then, would we want to emulate ageing by quitting sugar?

### SIGNS THAT YOUR METABOLISM IS ON THE DECLINE

- ✓ Low body temperature (increased sensitivity to cold, consistently cold hands and feet).
- ✓ Frequent urination.
- ✓ Digestive troubles (bloating after meals, delayed gastric emptying, less than one daily bowel movement).
- ✓ Poor sleep quality (insomnia, waking up during the night).
- ✓ Low sex drive or impaired sexual function (erectile dysfunction, vaginal dryness).
- ✓ Fertility issues.
- ✓ Absent, irregular or difficult periods (heavy, painful or abnormally long).
- ✓ Thinning hair or hair loss.
- ✓ Thin outer third of the eyebrows.
- ✓ Dry skin, especially on the hands and shins.
- ✓ Fatigue (feeling tired, sluggish or weak).
- ✓ Brain fog or poor mental focus.
- ✓ Mood disorders, increased anxiety or depression.
- ✓ Oedema (water retention), particularly facial puffiness.
- ✓ Weight gain.
- ✓ Muscle aches or weakness.

## CONCLUSION

The consequences of quitting sugar can be serious and far-reaching (and this list was by no means exhaustive). The irony is that the very thing that's being avoided will actually support metabolic function and long-term health. The *right* sugars will lower the stress hormones, feed the cells the glucose they need and support the production of thyroid hormone T3.

Only when stress hormones are low and metabolism is optimal will the body begin to self-regulate, regenerate, and function at its best. Improvements in digestion, detoxification, immune function, sleep quality, hormonal balance and reproductive health are certainly achievable, but hinge on properly incorporating sugars into the diet.

Don't Quit Sugar

# 2. Sugar Myths and Truths: Sorting Fact from Fiction

It's nearly impossible to decipher the deluge of nutritional information spruiked by today's media. Anti-sugar rhetoric is pervasive: we're told sugar causes obesity, diabetes and accelerated ageing, and that fructose is an unnecessary poison. With time and repetition, these myths are often accepted as fact and to question them becomes tantamount to heresy.

The reality is that the evidence is never black and white. Sugar research is often irrelevant to the human context or manipulated to justify a predetermined viewpoint. Distinctions are rarely made between isolated or processed forms of sugar and sugar as it occurs naturally.

If we examine the literature thoroughly and through physiological and scientific lenses, it's plain to see that sugar is *not* inherently evil and that the sugar myths are exactly that – myths.

The following section analyses and debunks some of the very dangerous illusions surrounding sugar. Buckle your seatbelts!

## MYTH: HUMANS HAVEN'T EVOLVED TO EAT SUGAR

This is really the most basic of all anti-sugar arguments, and it stems from two lines of thought. First, that protein and fat are preferential fuel sources for the body, which the previous chapter has disproven beyond doubt. Second, that human evolution has been characterised by diets low in sugar. However, even a cursory glance through our evolutionary history reveals this to be far from the truth …

More than 60 million years ago, the earliest living primates subsisted on fruits, leaves and insects. Humans' closest primate relatives – chimpanzees and bonobos – to this day obtain most of their energy from fruit.

Pre-humans were first able to deviate from the fruit-centric primate diet approximately 2.6 million years ago. At this time, the development of stone tools and, therefore, the ability to hunt introduced animal foods to the diet. Note that this was in addition to, *not* at the exclusion of fruits, leaves and insects.

The next two million years saw the advent of fire for cooking, and the addition of starchy vegetables as a source of nutrition. Thus, early human diets likely consisted of fruit, leaves, insects, honey, meat, fish, and starchy roots and tubers.

Modern hunter-gatherers continue to eat fruit and honey plentifully, particularly in temperate and equatorial regions. For the Hadza hunter-gatherers of Tanzania and the !Kung hunter-gatherers of the Kalahari Desert, fruit and honey form the basis of the diet. Both groups are lean.

On the Melanesian island of Kitava, around 70% of calories come from starchy root vegetables (taro, sweet potato, cassava) and fruit (banana, papaya, pineapple, mango, guava, watermelon, breadfruit). Kitavans are lean, with low fasting insulin levels and an undetectable incidence of diabetes, heart attack or stroke.

In Papua New Guinea, the Tukisenta consume 94% of calories in the form of starch (mostly sweet potato, which is also high in sucrose), yet they similarly have exceptional glucose tolerance and no evidence of diabetes.

*Our ancestors have been eating sugar – in the form of fruit, honey and root vegetables – throughout our evolution, and traditional diets today still emulate this pattern.*

Certainly, there are also traditional diets that rely heavily on animal products, and this is a testament to the innate adaptability of the human body. A tolerance for varying macronutrient ratios has been integral to our survival in diverse geographical locations and climates over time.

However, there are a few points worth noting. The Maasai of Africa consume large amounts of protein and fat in the form of raw meat and animal blood. But their diet is also centred on raw milk, which has a substantial natural sugar component.

The Arctic Inuit likewise survive on meat and fat, but with no milk and very little in the way of fruit, vegetables or natural sugar. Such a low-sugar diet is not conducive to reproduction, and it has been observed first-hand that the Inuit were traditionally required to supplement their diet with moose thyroid glands in order to conceive. (As we know, thyroid hormones and a high metabolism are both necessary for optimal reproductive function, and these depend on the cells receiving adequate sugar energy.)

More recently, the popular Paleo diet has advocated following in the ways of our hunter-gatherer ancestors. For the most part, this is a responsible recommendation in that it eliminates processed foods and instead focuses on nutrient-dense whole foods. But problems arise when Paleo advocates use modern (and typically inaccurate) scientific data – say, regarding fructose – to conjure arguments against fruit and root-vegetable sugar consumption.

Common anti-fruit arguments declare that hunter-gatherers would have had only seasonal access to fruit, or that ancient fruit was sour and not hybridised for sweetness like fruit today. These claims are unfounded and often lead Paleo followers down the dangerous road of sugar restriction. (Interestingly, wild fruit varieties are evidenced to contain higher amounts of fructose than cultivated fruits – 20–40% versus 10–30% of total sugar content, respectively.)

As I've described, whole-food sources of sugar have been an integral component of the human diet for longer than we've been human. If we weren't adapted to eating, metabolising and *thriving* on the glucose and (gasp!) fructose they contain, we most definitely wouldn't be here today to argue the point.

## MYTH: SUGAR CAUSES FAT GAIN

In the obesity blame-game, sugar has become a major scapegoat. Just as saturated fat was blasphemed in the 1980s (it has since been exonerated and proven *beneficial*), sugar today bears the brunt of media condemnation for its supposed 'fattening' quality.

Body fat accumulation cannot be ascribed to a single nutrient. This is a reductionist view and does not account for the intricate web of metabolic, nervous system and hormonal responses which function collaboratively to regulate food intake, energy storage and energy expenditure on a daily basis.

Nevertheless, it's important to properly examine the evidence.

Don't Quit Sugar

If sugar was inherently fattening, studies would reveal a strong association between high-sugar diets and levels of body fat. In reality, the opposite appears to be true.

Observational studies consistently show an *inverse* association between sugar intake and body mass index (BMI) – that is, as sugar increases as a proportion of daily calories, BMI trends downwards. This echoes the previous discussion of traditional cultures, all of whom were (or are) characteristically lean despite diets high in sugar.

*Controlled* studies in humans, which represent the gold standard in scientific research, time and again bear similar results. In one classic study, participants ate only fruit, sugar, honey, avocado and a small quantity of nuts for a period of six months. Fruit represented 82% of total energy intake, which – at a daily minimum allowance of 2400 calories – was by no means restrictive. Participants who were overweight lost weight, and those who were lean remained lean; all reported increases in energy and stamina.

In another study, overweight participants replaced a quarter of their daily fat intake with sugar in the form of sucrose, or starch. The diet was *not* calorie-restricted, and yet after six months, all participants had maintained or lost weight.

Elsewhere, it has been shown that low-calorie diets high in sugar (and predominantly refined sugar) still facilitate significant weight loss.

Let's take a look at the physiology.

A healthy body *does not* readily convert sugar to fat. If sugar is not immediately oxidised for energy, it is turned into glycogen and stored in the liver and muscles for later use (for example, during exercise). Sugar-to-fat conversion – termed **de novo lipogenesis (DNL)** – is metabolically expensive and our body does its utmost to avoid it.

*De novo lipogenesis: de novo – new; lipo – lipid (fat); genesis – creation.*

In response to high sugar consumption:

◈ Glycogen stores will expand significantly. Normally, whole-body glycogen is maintained at 250–500g. This can increase by an additional 500g to accommodate extra glucose.
◈ Thyroid hormone T4 will be more efficiently converted to active thyroid hormone T3.
◈ The cells will ramp up energy production (we're talking full-throttle sugar oxidation).
◈ Thermogenesis will increase and we'll get really, really warm.

It is only when these pathways become saturated that DNL occurs in *trivial amounts* (and by *trivial*, I mean maximal rates of 1–2%). This has been confirmed by multiple overfeeding studies and an isotopic tracer study, which is capable of measuring exact rates of DNL.

The only instance in which sugar *can be* problematic is when it is used to increase the palatability and energy density of processed foods. High palatability encourages overfeeding, often inadvertently. For example, studies show that individuals who regularly consume soft drinks (soda) tend not to compensate by reducing their food intake elsewhere. Fat gain then results from a *chronic energy surplus*, not sugar itself.

I certainly don't condone regular consumption of processed foods. Whole food sources of sugar – for example, fruit and sweet root vegetables – are difficult to eat in excess; the fibre and nutrients they contain stimulate homeostatic mechanisms which naturally regulate intake.

## WHAT ABOUT INSULIN?

**Insulin** is a hormone secreted by the pancreas as an entirely *normal* and *necessary* response to food consumption. Its primary role is to shuttle glucose, protein and fat out of the bloodstream and into the cells.

Unbeknown to many, **sugar is *not* the only insulin stimulant**: protein-rich foods often stimulate insulin to an equal or greater degree. For example, beef is just as insulinogenic (that is, it stimulates similar levels of insulin production) as pasta, while milk (and particularly whey protein) has been shown to stimulate *more* insulin than white bread.

Many people adhere to low-sugar, higher-protein diets in order to avoid insulin and insulin spikes, which is – ultimately – rather ironic.

The widespread (and misguided) fear is that insulin drives fat storage. When insulin is elevated, it *does* temporarily suppress the body's ability to burn fat (it is, after all, a signal of food/nutrient abundance). But this does not mean that it causes overall fat gain. There are a number of other factors at play:

- ❖ Insulin is co-secreted with the hormones **amylin** and **GLP-1**, both of which have been shown to *curb* food intake and *reduce* body weight.
- ❖ High-insulinogenic foods produce **increased satiety** (insulin and the satiety hormone **leptin** are thought to hold overlapping functions).
- ❖ Higher fasting insulin is associated with higher **resting energy expenditure** (independent of body fatness). If insulin promoted fat storage, then the opposite would be true.
- ❖ Experiments which block insulin receptors in the brain *increase* fat mass, which suggests a role of insulin in *constraining* fat.

Prospective studies typically show *no* correlation between insulin levels (both basal and post-meal) and increases in body fat over time. As is the case with sugar, it's myopic to pinpoint a single nutrient (or, in this case, hormone) as the sole mechanism for fat accumulation.

## MYTH: SUGAR CAUSES DIABETES

This is a huge myth to tackle in only so many words, because the perception of diabetes as a 'sugar disease' is so heavily ingrained.

Let's start with the basics.

In a healthy body, blood sugar levels are tightly regulated. When sugar is eaten and blood sugar rises, the pancreas secretes insulin, which signals for the cells to remove excess sugar from the blood. Healthy cells are **insulin sensitive** and will take up sugar to be used as energy or put into storage.

In diabetes, cells become **insulin resistant**. The pancreas still secretes insulin, but the cells fail to respond to its signal. Consequently, sugar remains in the blood, oversaturates it, and causes a state of **high blood sugar**.

The prevailing myth is that constantly eating sugar, and therefore constantly triggering insulin, is what makes the cells less sensitive to it over time. Diabetes in this way becomes seen as a disease of 'sugar excess', and the approach is to start monitoring or restricting sugar intake so as to avoid insulin spikes.

This couldn't be further from the truth.

A different (and more logical) approach shifts focus to *cell function*. Could damage to the cells be the problem? Is there some additional factor which might prevent sugar from getting into the cell?

Here, evidence overwhelmingly points to fatty acids – and particularly PUFA.

Don't Quit Sugar

- In a process called the *Randle cycle*, fat metabolism suppresses sugar metabolism. Put simply, high levels of fat in the bloodstream can block sugar from entering cells and being used as energy.
- Elevated circulating free fatty acids accumulate inside the cells, oxidise and produce inflammation. This degrades cell insulin receptors, reduces insulin sensitivity and prevents sugar uptake.
- In people who are overweight or obese, PUFA in visceral fat (this is the dangerous fat which surrounds the organs internally) have direct access to the liver via the portal vein. Thus, PUFA can damage the liver cells, leading to liver insulin resistance.
- Fatty acid metabolism increases the production of **lactate**, which can interfere with insulin signalling.

Diets which promote the use of fat for fuel (low-sugar, low-carb, etc.) increase the proportion of fatty acids in the bloodstream and therefore cell exposure to PUFA. Separate to diet, high levels of stress, impaired thyroid function and low metabolism will also encourage a reliance on fat for fuel.

The focus of diabetes prevention and treatment should first be on eliminating or ameliorating each of these potential contributors. Minimising fatty acids in the bloodstream allows for glucose metabolism to be restored and, with it, an increased ability of the cells to take up and utilise sugar.

Interestingly, **fructose** is the most beneficial sugar for diabetic recovery. And no, that's not a misprint. I'll get into the details once we debunk fructophobia.

## MYTH: FRUCTOPHOBIA

There seems to be no greater fear among the anti-sugar pundits than that of fructose. Anti-fructose hysteria – popularised only in the last four years – implicates fructose in **weight gain**, **insulin resistance**, **reduced appetite suppression** and **non-alcoholic fatty liver disease**. The message imparted is extreme – fructose is labelled as poisonous and addictive, analogous to alcohol or cocaine.

Anti-fructose proponents claim that when we eat fructose, it is immediately converted to fat in the liver through de novo lipogenesis (DNL). As proof, they rely on data from experiments in mice.

There are two problems here:

1. Mice convert sugar to fat extremely efficiently. Even on calorie-controlled diets, mice will produce fat from over 50% of the sugar they eat.
2. Experiments in mice typically use unrealistically large doses of fructose – we're talking up to 60% of total calories, which in humans would equate to drinking upwards of 5 litres of soft drink daily. In the US, average fructose intake sits at only 10% of daily calories; thus, there is a six-fold difference between what people are really eating and what research mice are being fed.

So, we've got excessive fructose intake combined with a metabolism that preferentially converts sugar to fat. **Of course we're going to see negative results!** On a high-fructose diet, mice experience high rates of DNL, which then causes weight gain, insulin resistance and fatty liver.

Do these results translate to humans? The answer is a resounding **no**.

Carefully controlled studies of human sugar metabolism have been able to track the passage of fructose once it enters the body. The majority of fructose is converted to glucose and only negligible amounts contribute to DNL. Humans simply do not experience the robust rate of fructose–fat conversion seen in mice.

Controlled feeding trials show *no* correlation between fructose consumption (as part of a balanced diet) and weight gain. In one study, participants **lost more weight** on a moderate-fructose diet than they did on a low-fructose diet.

What many people forget (or simply don't know) is that fructose stimulates thermogenesis (heat production) more so than glucose does. This means that when we eat fructose, a greater number of calories are immediately dissipated as heat by the body.

Fructose is only potentially fattening when it's consumed *in addition to* the normal diet. But this effect is equal to what would happen if excess calories were to come from any source.

Anti-sugar proponents often cite a second argument implicating fructose in weight gain: fructose alone does not trigger insulin or leptin, which are responsible for feelings of satiety. Supposedly then, eating fructose will lead to overeating.

Controlled studies in humans repeatedly show that fructose consumption *reduces* subsequent food intake. In a recent literature review, fructose was found to be no less satiating than other sources of sugar.

Such data, however, is largely irrelevant because fructose in food is *always* accompanied by an equal (or almost equal) measure of glucose. When fructose is consumed alongside glucose, there is a *controlled* secretion of insulin, which buffers against low blood sugar and thus the rapid return of hunger.

Indeed, when eaten in amounts normally obtained from fruit (around 10g per meal), fructose has been shown to **improve glycaemic control**.

This leads us to the idea of fructose as **advantageous in the treatment of insulin resistance and diabetes** (conditions in which glucose metabolism is impaired).

❖ Fructose, with no requirement for insulin, is able to enter the cells to be used as energy when glucose can't. Fructose enters the energy production pathway at a slightly different point to glucose, but the end result is still the same.
❖ Fructose stimulates the trapping of glucose inside the cells and also promotes glycogen synthesis. This clears glucose from the blood and downregulates gluconeogenesis (remember, insulin resistance in the liver cells causes uncontrolled glucose output).
❖ Fructose promotes glucose oxidation by activating two key enzymes, hepatic glucokinase and pyruvate dehydrogenase, both of which are inhibited in diabetes. Interestingly, hepatic glucokinase is a focus of new diabetes drug development research.
❖ In advanced diabetes, sucrose (glucose + fructose), together with coconut oil, has been shown to repair pancreatic beta cell function.

For diabetics, the common recommendation to consume grains and legumes is problematic. These break down exclusively to glucose, which – without the assistance of fructose – will likely remain in the bloodstream and perpetuate a state of high blood sugar.

In support, studies have shown that replacing complex carbohydrates with fructose increases insulin sensitivity, improves haemoglobin A1c, and lowers resting blood glucose levels.

Overwhelmingly, the evidence suggests that in insulin resistance and diabetes, moderate fructose intake, far from being 'toxic', is uniquely *beneficial*.

Don't Quit Sugar

## What about fatty liver?

If fructose–fat conversion in humans is negligible, then fructose cannot be the primary cause of non-alcoholic fatty liver disease (NAFLD).

Rather, what the research indicates is that the liver loses its ability to process fat (no matter the source) and then export it into the bloodstream. This causes fat to accumulate over time, producing a fatty liver.

The question, therefore, is what might damage the liver's ability to process fat? I could write a thesis on the subject (the research is vast and growing), but I'll give you a (very abridged) Cliffsnotes version.

## Choline deficiency

Liver fat metabolisation is dependent on the presence of the key nutrient **choline**. Diets deficient in choline have been shown to induce fatty liver, just as diets high in choline have been shown to protect against it.

Interestingly, the richest food source of choline – liver – has all but disappeared from the modern diet. Egg yolks – another excellent source – have suffered falls in consumption due to anti-cholesterol campaigns. For the vast majority of the population, choline intake sits far below current dietary recommendations.

## Insulin resistance

In insulin resistance and diabetes, we know that fats are more favourably metabolised over glucose. The breaking down of fats for energy increases the delivery of fatty acids to the liver. PUFA – on account of their toxicity and volatility – will cause oxidative stress and inflammation, which damages liver function. Fat can then accumulate and produce more inflammation in a vicious cycle.

## Exposure to endotoxin (endotoxemia)

Endotoxin is an internally produced toxin that resides in the lower intestine. Stress increases the absorption of endotoxin across the intestinal wall and into the bloodstream. (Remember: chronic stress weakens digestion and compromises intestinal barrier function.)

Evidence confirms that endotoxin can impair liver function and cause fat accumulation, particularly among overweight and obese individuals.

## Low thyroid function

Both insulin resistance and endotoxemia are products of low metabolism and impaired thyroid function. It's not surprising, then, that several studies have found a significant association between low thyroid function and NAFLD.

## MYTH: SUGAR PRODUCES AGES

Most people have heard of the acronym AGEs, most likely in relation to wrinkles or age spots (each of which is a manifestation of AGEs on the skin). Beyond this, a full understanding of their meaning and function often remains elusive. Let's break it down.

AGEs – or Advanced Glycation End products – are the result of rogue chemical reactions between sugars or PUFA, and proteins. In the body, they oxidise and cause tissue damage, which accelerates the ageing process and can lead to degenerative disease.

There are many misconceptions about AGEs, the biggest being that they are formed *only* through the interaction of **glucose** and proteins. The term **glycation** is derived from 'glucose', and this certainly promotes the misconception, but the truth is infinitely more complex.

AGEs are produced when glucose molecules bind to protein (or fat) molecules. This can occur inside the body (endogenously), or outside the body (exogenously) when we cook food – the browning of meat is a good example.

Fructose forms AGEs in a similar fashion, and in experimental settings is actually much more prone to do so than glucose. However, under normal physiological conditions in humans, there are only ever minuscule amounts of fructose in the blood, meaning that AGE formation is unlikely.

The greatest contributors to the body's AGE burden are PUFA. By nature, PUFA are highly unstable and easily oxidised (for example, through simple exposure to light, air and even modest heat). Within the body, the effects of oxidising PUFA are akin to shattering glass, with AGEs as shards that damage DNA and other protein molecules critical to cell function.

Research shows PUFA to be at least 10 times (and up to 23 times) more likely to produce AGEs than glucose. Thus, relying on fats for energy, which increases cell exposure to PUFA, is hazardous.

Two important compounds protect against AGE formation.

The first is **glutathione** – pronounced 'gloota-thigh-own' – which is known as the mother of all antioxidants. The body produces its own glutathione, but this is dependent on a robust metabolic rate, low PUFA levels and minimal stress.

The second is **carbon dioxide** ($CO_2$), which effectively shields proteins from the glycation process. Carbon dioxide is maximally generated through efficient sugar metabolism (burning fat for fuel produces much less $CO_2$ than glucose). Fructose, in particular, is $CO_2$-supportive.

In summary, to minimise AGE formation, we want to avoid PUFA (both through the diet and through using fat as a primary fuel source). To boost protection, we want to reduce stress and optimise metabolism, which requires including sugar in the diet.

### AGEs and Type 2 diabetes

AGE formation is known to be highest in people with diabetes. The near-sighted view implicates chronic high blood sugar (that is, increased glucose = increased potential AGEs). But high blood sugar is merely the symptom of defective energy metabolism and damaged cell function, which are – as we know – attributable to PUFA.

## MYTH: SUGAR FEEDS CANDIDA

Let's establish a simple truth right off the bat: **everyone has candida**.

Candida is a yeast-like fungus that normally resides on our skin and in our mucous membranes – these include the mouth, the vagina and the lower intestines.

An optimally functioning immune system will keep candida in check and curb its proliferation. In the intestines, immunoglobulin A (IgA) is the main antibody which protects against candida overgrowth.

When the immune system is weak, IgA secretion plummets, which enables candida to bloom unimpeded. Candida is opportunistic – without IgA's regulation, it will attempt to colonise all body tissues. This is when it becomes problematic.

*When metabolism is low and stress is high (as is the case in quitting sugar), immune function declines and IgA secretion is suppressed. The reliance on fat for fuel adds further insult – polyunsaturated fats have been shown to aggravate candida.*

Don't Quit Sugar

Being yeast-like, candida feeds on sugar. Anti-candida diets stipulate eliminating all sugar in order to 'starve' candida overgrowth. **But this is a band-aid approach which will ultimately cause more harm**.

Starved candida *needs* sugar and so will travel upwards through the intestines in search of it. If no sugar is found, candida will project invasive filaments into the intestinal wall, pass into the bloodstream, and – if not quickly destroyed by white blood cells – become systemic.

A better approach to candida overgrowth is to correct the underlying immune system suppression. For many people, this will require improving metabolism and moderating stress. The *right* sugars here are critical, not only as thyroid boosters and stress reducers, but also as fodder to prevent candida from becoming invasive.

# 3. Your How-to Guide to Sugar

Sugar in its natural form needs to be incorporated into the diet for optimal metabolic function and long-term health.

---

SUGAR:
- ❖ minimises stress hormone activity
- ❖ provides our cells with their preferred and most efficient source of energy
- ❖ replenishes liver glycogen, which facilitates the production of thyroid hormone T3.

---

Of course, I'm not suggesting you start mainlining maple syrup. As with everything, context and balance are key.

This section will provide answers regarding the **what, when and how of sugar consumption**.

I'm not going to be too prescriptive or set out a diet with 'rules' to abide by. Rather, I'll provide a collection of general principles, all aimed at reducing stress, maximising cellular glucose uptake and boosting thyroid activity.

How you decide to utilise these principles will depend on your body – your unique state of metabolic health, your current level of stress and your unique energy requirements.

For those who've previously restricted sugar, the aim should be to slowly and mindfully begin reintegrating it into the diet, and see where it takes you.

For those already eating sugar, the goal might shift to choosing better sources of sugar, or to eating sugar in a more targeted and purposeful manner.

For everyone, the end game is really to start making use of every eating opportunity to **nourish the body**, **boost metabolism** and **attain real and lasting health**.

So, without further ado …

## A SIMPLE LESSON IN SUGAR SCIENCE

Let's begin with a basic lesson in sugar science: how do sugars occur in food and how does the body break them down? (Feel free to skip over this if you're already well-versed in the topic.)

It's easiest to think of sugars as building blocks.

**Glucose** and **fructose** are each **monosaccharides**, or single sugar molecules (mono = one).

- G **Glucose** – as we know – is our cells' primary and preferred source of energy.
- F **Fructose** is derived from plants.

The third monosaccharide is galactose, which is only found in milk and milk products.

Su When glucose and fructose are bonded together, they form the **disaccharide** (di = two) **sucrose**.

Most natural sources of sugar are made up of glucose, fructose and/or sucrose in varying amounts.

There is a misconception that fruit contains only fructose. In truth, all fruit contains mostly sucrose, but also some free glucose and fructose as monosaccharides. As an example, one large peach contains approximately 8g sucrose, 3g glucose and 2g fructose.

$$Peach = \text{Su} + \text{Su} + \text{Su} +$$
$$\text{Su} + \text{Su} + \text{Su} + \text{Su} + \text{Su} +$$
$$\text{G} + \text{G} + \text{G} + \text{F} + \text{F}$$

The foods we know as **complex carbohydrates** – namely grains, legumes and potatoes – contain sugar in the form of starch.

**St** **Starch** is a **polysaccharide** (poly = many) made up of **many glucose molecules bonded together**.

$$\text{St} = \text{G G G G G G G G G}$$
$$\text{G G G G G G} \ldots$$

Disaccharides and polysaccharides cannot immediately be utilised by the body. To be of use, they need to be broken down into monosaccharides. This occurs during digestion.

When digestion is complete, it is the balance of the types of monosaccharides we're left with which determines how a food affects the body.

In a healthy person, the hormone insulin is released by the pancreas in response to food consumption.

Its role is to shuttle glucose out of the bloodstream and into the cells.

What we're aiming for is a steady and controlled insulin release with a corresponding steady and controlled rate of glucose uptake by properly functioning, insulin-sensitive cells.

- ❖ Glucose alone stimulates a rapid surge in insulin, which can result in glucose being cleared from the blood too quickly.
- ❖ Fructose does not stimulate insulin at all.
- ❖ When fructose is eaten and digested alongside glucose, **fructose moderates the stimulation of insulin by glucose**.

Thus, foods which contain a mix of glucose and fructose produce a steady rise in insulin and a steady rate of glucose uptake by the cells.

## THE BEST SOURCES OF SUGAR

Whole ripe fruits, well-cooked sweet root vegetables, orange juice, honey, maple syrup and molasses contain varying amounts of sucrose, free glucose and free fructose.

Whole fruits and root vegetables are most preferable because they also contain high concentrations of micronutrients and protective substances such as antioxidants.

In addition to modulating insulin, the simple sugars in these foods are digested in the upper section of the small intestine and do not usually cause digestive issues.

By contrast, the starches in whole grains, legumes and undercooked root vegetables are not fully broken down by the small intestine. Instead, they pass into the large intestine to produce gas and toxins, which can be problematic.

Starches, which break down exclusively to glucose, can also stimulate too much insulin too quickly, wreaking havoc on blood sugar levels.

The following pages offer a brief summary of the sugars most readily assimilated by the body to support energy production. Ideally, choose from these when preparing each of your meals and snacks.

Don't Quit Sugar

# Fruit

Fruit contains sugar in the form of **sucrose, glucose** and **fructose**, plus a wealth of vitamins, minerals, trace elements, phytochemicals and antioxidants.

The mix of glucose and fructose is ideal for blood sugar stability and is complemented by soluble fibre, which promotes satiety.

Studies show that when fruit is substituted for other sugars in the diet, there is increased weight loss and improved glycaemic control. Interestingly, the potassium in fruit mimics the function of insulin in the body. In this way, it can help shuttle glucose into the cells, which is especially important for those with diabetes.

A couple of caveats:

❖ **Eat only ripe fruits**. The sugars in ripe fruits are assimilated in the upper intestine and should not cause digestive issues. Improperly developed sugars in unripe fruits can pass into the lower intestine, where they will most likely ferment and cause gas, bloating and stomach pain.

❖ Apples and pears contain **pectin**, which can be hard to digest. Cooking breaks down pectin, so eat these fruits poached, stewed, baked or roasted.

# Root vegetables

Root vegetables contain **starch**, **sucrose**, **glucose** and **fructose** in varying quantities.

- **Beetroot** and **carrots** are much like fruit in that they contain mostly sucrose, with a little free glucose and fructose as monosaccharides.
- **Sweet potatoes** contain starch in addition to sucrose, free glucose and free fructose. Always eat them with a little fat (butter or coconut oil) to further moderate the insulin response.

Root vegetables are naturally anti-fungal, anti-bacterial and anti-parasitic – growing below ground, they need to protect themselves against fungi and nematodes. This protective quality is sustained when they are digested in the body; as they pass through the intestine, root vegetables will absorb and remove toxins and assist in balancing intestinal bacteria.

Carrots, in particular, should be eaten raw on a daily basis. Studies show them to be a natural antibiotic – carrot fibre stimulates bowel movement and prevents the absorption of toxins and other harmful substances in the intestinal tract.

TIP: With the exception of carrots, all root vegetables should be thoroughly cooked to ensure seamless and trouble-free digestion.

A note on the humble spud

Potatoes seem to get a bad rap as a high-carbohydrate 'comfort food'. It doesn't help that they are typically eaten deep-fried with a hefty dose of the toxic polyunsaturated oils.

But baked, boiled, steamed or stewed, potatoes are exceptionally healthful. Traditional cultures – particularly in South America – have consumed them as a primary source of calories for generations.

Potatoes:
- have a low calorie density and are highly satiating
- are high in quality, easily assimilated protein (vegans, take note!)
- contain substantial amounts of bio-available minerals, including magnesium, copper, potassium and manganese
- are an excellent source of vitamins C and B6
- rival broccoli and spinach in terms of their phytonutrient content.

# Orange juice

Orange juice is an excellent source of sugar (sucrose, glucose and fructose) for those with digestive issues who are unable to tolerate whole fruits or root vegetables.

Nutritional benefits include high levels of vitamin C, over 170 different phytonutrients, and more than 60 flavonoids, all of which have powerful anti-inflammatory and antioxidant effects.

In the clinical setting, orange juice has proven widely beneficial, with links to:

- improved insulin sensitivity
- lowered blood pressure
- decreased risk of diabetes
- decreased risk of cardiovascular disease
- reductions in several markers of inflammation, including C-reactive protein, TNF-a, IL-6, NF-kappaB and bacterial endotoxin.

TIP: In sensitive people, orange juice pulp can cause intestinal bloating. To avoid this, ensure you choose strained or pulp-free varieties (or better yet, juice and strain your own), and sip slowly alongside meals.

Don't Quit Sugar

# Dairy

Dairy has been a staple in the human diet for thousands of years. It is unique in that it is a complete food – it contains protein, fat and sugar, and is rich in micronutrients, most notably calcium and vitamins A, D, E and B. When digested and metabolised properly, it can effectively regulate blood sugar and reduce stress and inflammation in the body.

Unfortunately, dairy is today so often demonised: many argue that it's only meant for animals, or implicate it as a cause of allergies, acne and mucus production. In most cases, the issue is not dairy itself, but rather the **source of dairy** and the **health of the body consuming it**.

Consider the following:

- What are the cows being fed? In cows fed large amounts of grain, grain allergens can pass into their milk and trigger reactions in sensitive people (this is very much a case of 'we are what we eat').
- Are the cows being treated with hormones or antibiotics?
- Are thickeners being added to the milk or milk products? Most thickening agents – especially carrageenan – are powerful allergens which cause intestinal inflammation.
- If yogurt or cheese is being consumed, what types of cultures are used? Most generic brands utilise cheap fungi and bacteria which can aggravate digestive problems.
- Greek yogurt is high in protein and contains only small amounts of lactic acid, which can contribute to inflammation. Conventional yogurts are lower in protein and contain higher amounts of lactic acid.

*It's certainly worth investing in the best quality milk (and dairy products) you can find – preferably organic, and derived from cows, goats or sheep raised naturally on pasture.*

## Milk sugar

The sugar in milk is **lactose**, which is a **disaccharide of glucose and galactose**.

When our digestion is efficient, lactose is broken down and assimilated in the upper intestine via the **lactase enzyme**. 'Lactose intolerance' indicates that the intestine is no longer producing lactase.

Rather than avoiding lactose, it's desirable to restore lactase activity and the ability to digest lactose properly.

The commonly held belief is that the genes of some ethnic groups cause lactase production to fall in later life. However, reduced thyroid function, low metabolism, bacterial infections and progesterone deficiency can all also impede lactase activity. The correction of these conditions will often reinstate a tolerance of dairy products.

In people who are truly deficient in the lactase enzyme, daily consumption of small amounts of milk alongside meals can actually reinitiate lactase production and allow the body to slowly readapt to lactose digestion.

*When the body is stressed and in a low metabolic state, consuming too much dairy can increase acne and mucus production or cause digestive issues. In such cases, it's best to start with small amounts of high-quality cheese, such as mascarpone, ricotta or parmesan, which doesn't contain cultures. When these are well tolerated, milk can be introduced – in small amounts first, then increased over time.*

# Grains

**Whole grains** contain a number of **anti-nutrients** and **defensive substances** (toxins), which can impede digestion and block nutrient absorption. These include phytic acid, lectins, saponins, and protease or amylase inhibitors.

Healthy grain-eating populations typically soak, sprout, ferment and grind whole grains prior to cooking, or instead rely on **refined grains**, such as polished white rice.

⬧ Traditional preparation methods improve the digestibility of whole grains by reducing or eliminating toxins, lowering phytic acid content and increasing vitamin bioavailability.

⬧ Refined grains have had their outer layer (bran) removed and so do not contain toxins or anti-nutrients.

Properly prepared and refined grains have been part of the human diet since the onset of agriculture approximately 12 000 years ago. In this time, our bodies have undergone **genetic and epigenetic adaptations** which have improved our tolerance for grain consumption (this is particularly true for individuals of European lineage).

If grains do not cause you digestive distress, it's fine to include them as a source of sugar (starch) in your diet **in moderate amounts**. However, fruits and root vegetables will always be preferable because they are infinitely richer in micronutrients and protective substances such as antioxidants.

---

TIP: Choose refined grains (white rice or rice noodles are the most benign) or traditionally prepared whole grains, such as quality sourdough or sprouted-grain varieties of bread.

---

Don't Quit Sugar

# Medjool dates

Yes, dates are technically a fruit, but they deserve a special mention. Date palm trees date back to the Old Stone Age period in the Middle East; medjool dates have been coveted as both a food and a healing source for thousands of years.

Dates are nutritional powerhouses and are particularly high in B vitamins and the minerals potassium, magnesium, copper and manganese. Sugars are mostly in the form of free glucose and fructose, with tiny amounts of sucrose.

TIP: As an alternative to honey or maple syrup, blend soaked dates with water to form a delicious 'date syrup'.

# Honey

Honey contains equal parts glucose and fructose. When raw and unprocessed, it has been found to contain up to 180 protective substances – these are anti-inflammatory, anti-bacterial and improve immunity.

TIP: Make sure the honey you buy is raw and untreated.

# Maple syrup

Maple syrup is produced from the sap of the maple tree. Its sugar is mostly in the form of sucrose, with some free glucose and only small amounts of free fructose.

It contains higher concentrations of minerals than honey, particularly zinc and manganese. Zinc is critical for optimal immune function. Manganese is a cofactor in several enzymes which protect against oxidative damage.

TIP: Look for pure, Grade B maple syrup.

# Molasses

Molasses is the dark liquid by-product of refining sugarcane into granulated sugar. It is robust in flavour and mineral-rich – just 1 tablespoon contains up to 20% of the recommended daily intake of calcium, copper, manganese, potassium and magnesium.

# Granulated cane sugar

Granulated sugar is produced through boiling and then crystallising sugarcane syrup. Nutritionally speaking, there isn't much difference between the various sizes and types of sugar granules. White (table) sugar, caster sugar and icing sugar are all pure sucrose; raw (Turbinado) sugar and brown sugar are just sucrose with trace amounts of molasses. All contain the same amount of energy and break down to equal parts glucose and fructose in the body.

# Palm sugar

Popular in Thai, Indonesian and Indian cooking, palm sugar derives from the sap of various species of palm tree. Like cane sugar, it is produced through a process of boiling and crystallisation.

Coconut palm sugar is becoming increasingly popular in nutrition circles. It naturally contains small amounts of vitamins B1, B2, B3 and B6 and the minerals zinc and potassium. Chemically, however, it is predominantly sucrose and is comparable to cane sugar once it enters the body.

Don't Quit Sugar

## A FEW NOTES ON SUGAR ALTERNATIVES

- The vast majority of **artificial sweeteners** cannot be broken down by the digestive system and are shunted to the liver for detoxification. The irony is that proper liver function relies on adequate *real sugar* stores in the form of glycogen. Without glycogen, efficient detoxification cannot take place and chemicals will remain in the liver, causing a toxic backload. By not eating real sugar, we damage the body's ability to handle fake sugars!

- **Rice syrup** is pure glucose. Used alone it will send insulin levels skyward, which can result in a statc of low blood sugar. Opt instead for honey or maple syrup, each of which has a balance of glucose and fructose.

- **Stevia** is natural and plant-derived. However, as a substitute for real sugar in the diet, it will always cause problems. Stevia tastes sweet, but provides no glucose or energy to the cells. This perpetuates low blood sugar, increases appetite and elevates the stress hormones (which are then forced to seek sugar from body structure).

- **High fructose corn syrup (HFCS)** is a highly refined (and very cheaply produced) sweetener derived from corn. Corn is first milled to yield corn starch, which is further processed to give corn syrup. Corn syrup is almost entirely glucose; to increase its sweetness, it undergoes more processing whereby some of its glucose is converted to fructose. The resulting HFCS is widely used in soft drinks, baked goods, cereals, condiments and processed foods, mostly in the US.

A recent study found HFCS to contain four to five times more sugar than previously thought. Thus, nutrition data for HFCS-containing soft drinks and food products could to this point have grossly underestimated their own sugar and calorie counts.

US consumption data shows a decrease in sucrose consumption since 1970, but an equal and parallel increase in HFCS consumption. Simply by switching sugar sources, the US population may have unknowingly and very dramatically increased their energy intake.

Regardless, natural sources of fructose will always be the superior choice. Relevant human studies, which include fructose in the forms of whole fruit and honey, time and again produce **positive** results both with regard to weight management and blood sugar regulation.

# Principle 1:

## BALANCE BLOOD SUGAR

A drop in blood sugar can signal the release of the stress hormones. Stabilising blood sugar will therefore minimise stress and ensure a continual and even supply of glucose to the cells.

Advocates of low- and no-sugar diets often brag about their own 'blood sugar stability' despite not eating sugar. In reality, a state of **chronic low blood sugar** is being ameliorated by chronically high levels of cortisol, which breaks down tissue protein to raise blood sugar.

The first principle of *real* blood sugar stabilisation is to **consume all three macronutrients in combination – that is, protein, sugar and fat**. Why?

⇩ Protein pulls blood sugar down.

⇧ Sugar pushes blood sugar up.

~ Fat slows the entry of sugar and protein into the bloodstream.

❖ **Protein stimulates insulin**, which signals for our muscle cells to assimilate amino acids. If sugar isn't eaten to balance protein, insulin will pull sugar out of the blood, causing a sharp drop in blood sugar.

❖ **Starches**, which break down exclusively to glucose, also stimulate insulin, and can result in sugar being cleared from the blood too quickly.

❖ Sugars that contain a **mix of glucose and fructose** – fruit, honey, beetroot, sweet potato – are most preferable for blood sugar control. Fructose does not stimulate insulin and so attenuates the rise in insulin generated by glucose and protein.

❖ If you're eating a meal high in starch, including a piece of fruit for dessert will provide fructose to offset the starch's glucose.

As a general guideline for stable blood sugar, meals should contain more sugar than protein and more protein than fat.

*Sugar > protein > fat*

How much sugar should you eat?
As a bare minimum for a sedentary person, consider the following:

❖ The brain alone consumes 80–100g of glucose every day.

❖ The liver can store up to around 120g of glucose, and this is made accessible to our organs, cells and the central nervous system when (not if) they require it. Liver glycogen stores need to be replenished on a **daily basis**.

Of course, someone who exercises regularly or has a high level of incidental activity will obviously require more sugar (and overall food intake) than someone who is largely sedentary.

Don't Quit Sugar

## Sugar cravings

Sugar cravings (or the tendency to overeat) can – in most cases – be ascribed to blood sugar mismanagement. When cravings strike, most people reach for starch-based foods – think muesli bars, chips, biscuits, muffins or banana bread – which are broken down predominantly to glucose. We know that starches alone send insulin levels skyward: too quickly, sugar is cleared from the bloodstream, leaving us with low blood sugar. Low blood sugar makes us crave more sugar, initiating the cycle again. This is the blood sugar rollercoaster.

The solution? Always eat to balance blood sugar. Opt for fruit (or another source of sucrose) over starch and always combine it with protein and fat.

Low- and no-sugar dieters typically satiate sugar cravings with more and more fat. But remember, the more our cells burn fat for fuel, the harder it becomes to burn glucose and the greater the likelihood of developing insulin resistance.

# Principle 2:

## NEVER SKIP BREAKFAST

Cortisol tends to peak between 6 and 7 am, and glycogen stores need replenishing after the nightly fast, so skipping breakfast is not a good idea!

If you wake up with no appetite, it's very likely your stress hormones are sky-high. To immediately downregulate the stress hormones, sip on a small glass of salted orange juice. The combination of sugar and salt is the best stress buster. (There's a reason trauma patients are given IVs containing sugar and salt!)

Try to eat a balanced breakfast as soon as you can (within 30 minutes of waking is ideal). Easily digestible sugars, quality protein and a little saturated fat will replenish glycogen, balance blood sugar and provide sustained energy through the morning.

TIPS:

❖ Never drink coffee alone or on an empty stomach. This will increase adrenaline (the coffee 'high') and lower blood sugar.

❖ **Coffee** can certainly be included in the diet – it is high in nutrients (magnesium, vitamin B1) and a powerful thyroid booster. To avoid the adrenaline spike, it is best to drink it with full-fat milk, cream or coconut milk, and to sip it slowly alongside meals.

❖ **Eggs** are a quick and convenient breakfast option. However, they tend to lower blood sugar more so than other sources of protein (they stimulate a greater insulin response). To compensate, simply increase your ratio of sugar to protein whenever eggs are eaten. For example, accompany eggs with a piece of fruit and a tall glass of orange juice.

Don't Quit Sugar

# Principle 3:

## EAT REGULAR MEALS

In order to prevent a drop in blood sugar, it's important to eat regular, balanced meals. **Make food a priority**.

The length of time you're able to go between meals will depend on your level of metabolic health. Those with an optimal metabolism are able to properly store sugar as liver glycogen, which can be liberated between meals to balance blood sugar and provide energy.

If you're metabolically challenged, or coming off a low-sugar diet, the liver's ability to store sugar is usually compromised (remember, high stress and fats in the bloodstream block glucose from entering the cells). Therefore, more frequent meals are often necessary to balance blood sugar.

In such a state, **reteaching the liver to store sugar** becomes a priority. Eating foods with a mix of glucose and fructose (fruit, honey, beetroot, sweet potato) is helpful. Fructose is able to shuttle glucose into the liver cells, and improves the cells' ability to utilise glucose for energy production.

It is only when the liver is able to properly store sugar as glycogen that efficient conversion of thyroid hormone T4 to thyroid hormone T3 can take place.

If at any point during the day you start experiencing signs of low blood sugar:

❖ immediately eat or drink something sugary and salty – as on waking, a small glass of salted orange juice is a good option
❖ follow with a balanced snack as soon as you can – my favourite is a hunk of quality cheese with a piece of fruit.

Signs of low blood sugar: *cold hands and feet, frequent urination (especially if the urine is colourless), irritability, anxiety, shakiness, sugar cravings, lethargy and headaches.*

A NOTE ON FLUIDS

If your metabolism is low or you are prone to low blood sugar, it's important to monitor your fluid intake. Many people habitually consume excessive amounts of water, coffee or tea throughout the day. This can exacerbate low blood sugar (too much fluid dilutes cellular sugar content) and simultaneously mask its symptoms (by providing a false sense of 'fullness'). If you're urinating frequently – more than once every few hours – or if your urine is clear in colour, you're most likely taking in too much fluid.

# Principle 4:

## IF YOU HAVE TROUBLE SLEEPING, EAT A BEDTIME SNACK

When metabolism is optimal, restful and uninterrupted sleep should come easily.

If you awaken during the night or suffer from insomnia, it's likely you're in a low metabolic state, with high stress hormone activity and a drop in blood sugar during the sleeping hours.

Most people awaken between 1 and 4 am, when adrenaline peaks. The lower your metabolism, the higher the adrenaline peak and the greater the likelihood of experiencing additional symptoms – anxiety, a racing mind and heart palpitations are common.

By eating something sugary and salty before bed, and again during the night if you awaken, it's possible to lower adrenaline and balance blood sugar.

❖ Ripe fruits and salted orange juice are good choices. In addition to sugar, fruit contains the anti-stress minerals magnesium and potassium, which boost energy production and benefit sleep quality. Add a small chunk of cheese or a cup of bone broth for additional salt and protein.
❖ Warm milk with honey and a pinch of salt is the ultimate sleep tonic. Calcium reduces stress, is extremely pro-metabolic and decreases levels of parathyroid hormone, which can play a role in insomnia.

*Never* eat a high-protein dinner unbalanced by sugars. As I've mentioned, protein alone will stimulate insulin, lower blood sugar and precipitate a rise in stress hormones. Always offset protein-heavy dinners with sugars from sweet root vegetables, a little rice or potato, and, ideally, a piece of fruit for dessert.

Consistent restful sleep will only come about with consistent blood sugar balance, decreased stress hormones, and, ultimately, an increase in the body's metabolic rate.

FACT: Serotonin and melatonin have each developed reputations as sleep-inducers. In actuality, these hormones are associated with stress, inflammation and low metabolism. Therefore, they are not conducive to restful sleep, but rather can aggravate sleep issues. Use food as your supplement instead!

# Principle 5:

## DON'T FEAR FRUCTOSE

Anti-fructose propaganda has produced a culture of extreme and unwarranted fructose alarmism. But in the context of a balanced diet, and when consumed as a component of *natural* foods, **fructose is certainly nothing to fear**.

* Foods which contain a balance of glucose and fructose are ideal for **blood sugar control**. Fructose, as we know, does *not* stimulate insulin, and so modulates the rise in insulin produced by glucose. The result is a slower (and steadier) release of sugar into the bloodstream. Ripe fruits or well-cooked beetroot (which contains sucrose, glucose and fructose) are perfect, always balanced by protein and fat.
* If your metabolism is low and you are slightly **insulin resistant**, fructose can be especially helpful towards restoring proper glucose metabolism.

Remember, a low-metabolic, high-stress state is associated with fatty acid oxidation. Adrenaline liberates fatty acids from the body's fat stores, which can accumulate inside the cells, oxidise and damage cellular insulin sensitivity.

* Fructose, without the need for insulin, can enter the cells to be used as energy when glucose can't. Fructose molecules are able to 'piggyback' glucose molecules into the cells and can stimulate both glycogen synthesis and glucose oxidation.

    Again, foods with a balance of glucose and fructose are most preferable. In a state of insulin resistance, starch has a tendency to send blood sugar skyward.

* With regard to **weight loss**, fructose may hold a competitive advantage. Fructose stimulates thermogenesis more so than glucose, meaning that a greater number of calories are immediately dissipated as heat. Ripe fruits are your best bet – the soluble fibre promotes satiety, and the vitamin, mineral and antioxidant content trumps even root vegetables on a calorie-for-calorie basis.

## How much fructose?

Inevitably, the question arises: how much fructose is too much?

Relevant *human* studies have demonstrated no issue with daily intakes in the range of 60–100g for sedentary people. To provide some perspective, 60g of fructose equates to **three whole rockmelons** (cantaloupes), **12 peaches** or **20 small beets**.

In the context of a whole-foods diet, agonising over fructose allowances is therefore rather gratuitous.

Enjoy fruits, root vegetables and even a little sugar syrup (honey, molasses, maple syrup) for the nourishment and metabolic benefit they afford, and discard any fructose fear!

## Fructose and foetal development

Fructose plays a significant role in reproduction and foetal development.

For men, it is the main sugar in the seminal fluid (semen). In fact, sperm motility has been shown to depend on their ability to convert fructose into energy.

In the first stages of pregnancy, the intrauterine environment remains low in oxygen until the placenta is fully functional and glucose becomes the primary source of energy for the foetus. In the interim, fructose – which is present in high concentrations – facilitates important chemical reactions and energy production.

Once the placenta has developed, it converts some glucose from the mother's blood into fructose. Fructose from the mother's blood is also transferred freely to the foetus, where it promotes and maintains cellular health.

Indeed, fructose metabolism is present and active from the earliest stages of human life.

FACT: Glucose and fructose account for approximately 80% of foetal energy consumption. For mums, maintaining adequate liver glycogen stores is therefore imperative (don't quit sugar!). If the liver isn't energised, it is unable to properly detoxify excess oestrogen. Excess oestrogen (relative to progesterone) can cause a spasming of the bile duct (attached to the small intestine), increasing the likelihood and severity of morning sickness.

Don't Quit Sugar

# Principle 6:

## GET TO KNOW YOUR BODY

How can you tell if your metabolism is optimal or compromised? Are there signs of high stress hormone activity?

The most basic indicators of metabolic health are **body temperature** and **heart rate**.

- ❖ On waking, armpit or under-the-tongue temperature should read a minimum 36.6°C (97.8°F), and should steadily rise to 37.0°C (98.6°F) during the course of the day.
- ❖ Hands, feet and nose should be consistently warm (without the need for gloves or multiple pairs of socks!).
- ❖ Resting heart rate should be in the range of 70–85 beats per minute at all times.

If your waking temperature and heart rate are below ideal, it's likely your metabolism is low – stressed cells conserve energy instead of pumping it out at full capacity.

### Your game plan?

Read and reread this chapter (including the delicious meal and snack ideas, which follow), then slowly – at your own pace – begin mindfully integrating (or reintegrating) sugar into your diet as I've described.

If your food choices are on target, your temperature and heart rate should rise slightly in response to each meal.

If they remain consistently low, increase your ratio of sugar to protein or experiment with different *types* of sugar – how do you react to fruit versus beetroot, sweet potato or rice? It's about getting to know **your body**, assessing its response to different foods and food quantities,

and adjusting and tweaking accordingly.

Eventually (within weeks or months, depending on your starting point), your waking temperature should start to trend upward as well (this is usually the last thing to fall into place).

---

It's easy to become obsessive about measuring your temperature and heart rate. Don't. I simply want you to be more aware of your body and its basic signals of biofeedback. Remember that this is a process. We're aiming for gradual – but very real – improvements in metabolism and health over time.

Also note that while sugar is integral to metabolic correction, there are several other factors which can help or hinder the journey. Stress reduction, sleep, decreasing polyunsaturated fat intake and, in most cases, increasing salt intake are all important.

---

# Principle 7:

## SUGAR AND EXERCISE GO HAND IN HAND

There's no arguing with the fact that we should all be physically active – we need to be on our feet, moving around and enjoyably engaging in daily life. Beyond this, formal exercise should only be undertaken as appropriate to your level of metabolic health.

Exercise, no matter how you look at it, is *stressful*.

❖ In an already stressed, metabolically compromised body, exercise will only be **catabolic** – that is, it will increase stress and further lower metabolism.

❖ In a healthy body, *acute stress* induced by the *right types* of exercise can be **anabolic** – it can build strength and support metabolism. Anaerobic activities – think resistance training or short, intense interval sprints – are most favourable. Aerobic activities, by contrast, are akin to *chronic stress* and will simply break the body down over time.

It's imperative to recognise that exercise increases energy demands; our food intake – and particularly our sugar intake – needs to reflect this.

To train smart and minimise stress:

❖ **Before exercise**, consume a combination of sugar and protein to balance blood sugar and spare muscle glycogen.

❖ **During exercise**, sip small amounts of a sugar-sweetened beverage (orange juice is ideal) to blunt a rise in cortisol and increase glucose oxidation.

❖ **After exercise**, again consume a combination of sugar and protein. This will stabilise blood sugar, replenish glycogen, encourage the disposal of lactic acid and stimulate muscle repair.

Attempting to exercise on a low- or no-sugar diet is a recipe for metabolic disaster. Inadequate glycogen will impair performance, and the stress hormones will go into overdrive; cortisol in particular will break down body tissue at an increased rate to balance blood sugar and fuel the body.

Don't Quit Sugar

# Principle 8:

## THE ONLY HEALTHY WAY TO LOSE WEIGHT

Low- and no-sugar diets are not the answer to sustainable weight loss. While an initial drop in body weight can be encouraging, this is largely attributable to a state of high stress and tissue breakdown.

Long-term, the picture is bleak. With poor thyroid function and a lowered metabolism, the body begins expending fewer and fewer calories on basic functions, including movement and exercise. As such, weight maintenance (or additional weight loss, if that is the goal) requires progressively less and less food intake or progressively more and more forced energy expenditure through stressful exercise.

The irony is that the more we restrict food, or the more we exercise the body, the higher our stress levels soar and the lower our metabolism falls. It's a vicious cycle and certainly no way to live.

Attaining and maintaining an ideal weight should be a natural consequence of low stress, adequate nutrition and, most significantly, a **properly functioning metabolism**.

Raising core (waking) temperature by 1°C has been associated with a 10–13% increase in metabolic rate. This means the body will effortlessly expend an additional 10–13% more calories per day, even if you're just lying in bed.

Weight loss certainly won't be as fast, but it will be lasting. And you'll get to eat abundantly, exercise without shackles (if and when you want to, because you enjoy it) and hang on to your health for the long haul.

Bottom line? Get healthy to lose weight. Don't set out to lose weight and expect to gain health.

# Recipes

The following recipes show you how to healthfully (and deliciously) combine natural sugars with proteins and fats for stress reduction, blood sugar control and sustained metabolic health.

I tend to favour the freshest possible, most nutrient-dense ingredients – in this way, supplementation (such as with multivitamins) becomes unnecessary.

Before reading the recipes you may like to consider the following:

- ❖ You'll see that most recipes include seasonal fruits and/or sweet root vegetables as primary sources of sugar. Why?
  - The balance of glucose and fructose is most preferable for blood sugar control.
  - When ripe and/or well cooked, fruits and root vegetables are easily digestible.
  - They contain higher concentrations of micronutrients and protective substances (for example, antioxidants) as compared with other sugars.
- ❖ In some recipes, starches (i.e. pure glucose) – sourdough bread, white potatoes, rice or rice noodles – are the only source of sugar. If you're insulin resistant, coming off a low-sugar diet or are prone to low blood sugar, limit these meals to occasionally, and always follow with a source of sucrose, such as fruit.
- ❖ Raw, unprocessed honey and maple syrup are used in small amounts to enhance sweetness when necessary. You could substitute pureed medjool dates, apple sauce or even orange juice.
- ❖ As a substitute for flour, I like to use rolled oats which have been ground to a powder in a food processor (I'll often process a big batch at a time so that I've always got some on hand).
- ❖ Many of the recipes – especially the breakfasts and some desserts (yes, you read that correctly) – can serve as snacks in smaller portions. This is because they are macronutrient-balanced and nutrient-dense.

## YOUR SHOPPING LIST

### Pantry staples

*Dry goods:* cocoa powder, coconut sugar, dark (70%) chocolate, dried figs (sulphur-free), dried prunes (sulphur-free), palm sugar, rice noodles, rolled oats, white rice.

*Liquids and condiments:* apple cider vinegar, balsamic vinegar, coconut milk, coconut oil, extra virgin olive oil, maple syrup, molasses, mustard, raw honey, red wine vinegar.

*Spices and herbs:* bay leaves, black peppercorns, chilli flakes, cinnamon (ground and whole sticks), cloves, coriander seed powder, cumin powder, curry powder, ground nutmeg, paprika (sweet and smoked), sea salt, star anise, turmeric, whole vanilla beans, vanilla extract.

*Jars and tins:* capers, capsicum (chargrilled in vinegar), gherkins, olives, tomatoes (tinned, passata [sieved], tomato paste).

## Fresh produce

*Seasonal fruit:* apples, apricots, bananas, blueberries, cherries, figs, grapes, honeydew melon, kiwifruit, mandarins, mangoes, medjool dates, nectarines, oranges, papaya, peaches, pears, persimmons, pineapple, plums, raspberries, rockmelon, watermelon.

*Vegetables:* beetroot, capsicum, carrots, corn, cucumber, eggplant, fresh herbs (basil, chives, coriander, mint, parsley, thyme), garlic, ginger, leeks, mushrooms, onion, parsnip, potato, pumpkin, sweet potato, tomato, yellow squash, zucchini.

*Proteins:* cheese (feta, ricotta, haloumi, parmesan), eggs (pasture-fed), fish (barramundi, cod, perch, snapper, swordfish, tuna), shellfish (prawns, oysters, scallops), Greek yogurt (full-fat),

Don't Quit Sugar

milk (whole, cow's and goat's), poultry (chicken), red meat (beef: bones, eye fillet, mince, stewing; lamb: shanks, chops, shoulder or leg).

*Fats:* butter, cream, olives.

## A FEW NOTES ON PROTEIN

I prefer animal sources of protein for their nutrient density and easy digestibility.

- If you can, buy **meat** and **dairy** from grass-fed animals and **eggs** from pastured (free-range) chickens. They contain higher levels of micronutrients and a more favourable fatty acid profile – including less toxic polyunsaturated fat – than grain-fed alternatives.
- Try to balance your intake of lean meats with flavourful braises, roasts and stews. Cooking meat on the bone intensifies flavour, reduces waste and provides a full spectrum of amino acids.

**Shellfish** and white-fleshed **fish** are an excellent source of minerals. Wild fish varieties are always preferable to farmed.

**Gelatin** is the cooked form of collagen found in the bones, skin and connective tissues of animals and fish. It is anti-inflammatory and extremely healing to the body. Several recipes utilise bone broth – a concentrated source of gelatin – or gelatin powder. I recommend Great Lakes beef gelatin powder, which is sourced from healthy, grass-fed cattle.

### GELATIN HAS BEEN SHOWN TO:

- repair the intestinal lining
- support skin, hair and nail health
- preserve bone strength and joint mobility
- protect against oxidative damage (free radicals)
- improve immune function
- encourage hydrochloric acid production, which is necessary for protein digestion
- increase the digestibility and utilisation of other proteins.

### MY FAVOURITE FATS

- For roasting, frying and sautéing, I recommend heat-stable saturated fats such as **coconut oil** and **butter**.
- **Extra virgin olive oil** is best drizzled onto salads. The monounsaturated fats it contains can degrade and oxidise when heated.
- Avoid **nut, seed** and **vegetable oils**. These contain the toxic polyunsaturated fatty acids, which – as we've learnt – promote stress, inflammation and insulin resistance and downregulate metabolism.
- **Coconut milk** and **dried coconut flesh** (desiccated, shredded or flaked) are additional sources of healthy saturated fat. When buying canned coconut milk, look for brands that contain only water and coconut as ingredients (in Australia, Ayam is great). Most canned coconut milk contains fillers and gums which can interfere with digestion and promote inflammation.
- **Dairy fat** – in whole milk, whole-milk cheeses and cream – is a fantastic source of fat-soluble vitamins, including vitamin A.

# BREAKFAST

A balanced breakfast will lower nocturnal stress hormones, replenish liver glycogen and stabilise blood sugar through the morning.

Combine eggs, Greek yogurt or ricotta (*protein, fat*) with seasonal fruit, potato, oats or sourdough (*natural sugar*) and a little coconut oil or butter, when needed.

# Little Baked Ricotta Cakes with Plums

ORGANIC RICOTTA IS THE PUREST CHEESE you can buy; it should contain only milk, vinegar and salt, and no enzymes or cultures, which can be allergenic in sensitive people. These little cakes are a perfect 'grab and go' breakfast option.

## INGREDIENTS

butter or coconut oil, for greasing
500g ricotta cheese
2 eggs
2 tbs raw honey
1 vanilla bean, halved lengthways
    and seeds scraped
6 plums, halved, stones removed
½ tsp orange zest
1 tbs orange juice

## METHOD

1. Preheat the oven to 180°C. Grease a 6 x ½-cup capacity muffin tin with butter or coconut oil.

2. Whisk together the ricotta, eggs, honey and half the vanilla seeds until smooth and creamy (this is easily done in a food processor or with electric beaters). Spoon the mixture into the prepared muffin tin.

3. Slice 2 plums into thin wedges and arrange on top of the ricotta, pressing down into the surface. Bake the cakes 25–30 minutes or until golden.

4. Meanwhile, finely chop the remaining plums and combine in a small bowl with the orange zest, juice and the remaining vanilla seeds.

5. Serve the ricotta cakes warm or at room temperature with the plum salsa to the side.

Makes 6.

Don't Quit Sugar

# Sweet Potato Tortilla

Traditional spanish tortilla transforms the humblest ingredients – potatoes, eggs, onions and olive oil – into a truly satisfying breakfast, lunch, dinner or tapas dish. For something different, I like to use sweet potato. (I also replace the olive oil with coconut oil, which doesn't degrade when heated.)

## INGREDIENTS

2 tbs coconut oil
1 medium brown onion, halved and finely sliced
2 medium sweet potatoes, skin on, sliced into 5mm rounds
5 eggs, beaten
1 tbs finely chopped flat-leaf parsley, plus extra to serve
1 tsp sweet paprika
sea salt and freshly ground black pepper

## METHOD

1. Preheat the oven to 180°C. Bring a large pot of salted water to the boil and add the sweet potato slices. Cook for 4–5 minutes, until just tender. Drain well.

2. Meanwhile, melt 1 tablespoon of coconut oil in a medium ovenproof frying pan over medium-high heat. Sauté the onion for 5–10 minutes, until softened but not browned. Remove from the heat.

3. In a large bowl, combine the sweet potato slices, sautéed onion, eggs, parsley and paprika. Season generously with salt and pepper.

4. Melt the remaining tablespoon of coconut oil in the frying pan. Add the sweet potato mixture, using a spatula to distribute it evenly and flatten the surface. Bake for 25–30 minutes, until golden brown and cooked through. Scatter with parsley and serve sliced into thick wedges.

Leftover tortilla is an excellent (and easily portable) snack or lunch option.

# Two-Tone Coconut Jelly with Mango

THIS BREAKFAST IS DAIRY-FREE AND EGG-FREE, but still provides easily assimilable protein by way of gelatin. If you don't have access to the Great Lakes variety, substitute another quality beef gelatin and adjust the required amount according to packet instructions.

## INGREDIENTS

¼ cup, plus 1 tbs Great Lakes beef gelatin

4 cups (1L) young coconut water (3–4 coconuts)*

400ml can coconut milk, shaken well

2 medium mangoes, skin removed and thinly sliced

## METHOD

1. In a medium saucepan, whisk together ¼ cup of gelatin and 1 cup of coconut water. Place over low heat and whisk until the gelatin has dissolved. Add the remaining 3 cups of coconut water and whisk thoroughly to combine. Divide the mixture between four small bowls and chill in the refrigerator until set.

2. In the same saucepan, whisk together the remaining tablespoon of gelatin and the coconut milk. Again, place over low heat and whisk until the gelatin has dissolved. Pour the mixture in an even layer on top of the coconut water jellies. Chill in the refrigerator until set.

3. To serve, top each bowl of jelly with slices of mango.

Makes 4.

---

The jellies will keep in the fridge for several days and are great to have on hand for the weekday morning rush.

*Try to get your hands on young whole Thai coconuts, now generally available in greengrocers and major supermarkets. You'll need a large knife to puncture the tops in order to extract the sweet water within. If Thai coconuts aren't available, substitute bottled (Tetra-Pak) pure coconut water without additives.

---

Don't Quit Sugar

# Flour-Free Carrot Cake Pancakes

GRATED CARROT FUNCTIONS AS AN INTESTINAL 'broom'; its unique fibre is able to bind toxins for elimination and reduce inflammation. These pancakes borrow the flavours of the classic cake but are flour- and dairy-free. Top with yogurt, ricotta, a handful of sultanas or an indulgent drizzle of maple syrup.

## INGREDIENTS

4 eggs
¾ cup mashed banana (about
    2 medium bananas)
1 cup grated carrot
½ cup desiccated (finely shredded)
    coconut
¼ cup sultanas, plus extra to serve
1 tsp cinnamon
¼ tsp ground nutmeg
1 tsp baking powder
coconut oil or butter, for greasing
yogurt, ricotta or maple syrup, to
    serve

## METHOD

1. In a large bowl, whisk together the eggs, banana, carrot and coconut. Stir through the sultanas, cinnamon, nutmeg and baking powder.

2. Grease a large frying pan with coconut oil or butter and heat over medium heat.

3. Using a heaped tablespoon of batter for each pancake, cook for 2–3 minutes on each side, until golden brown and cooked through. Serve with toppings of your choice.

Serves 2.

# Puffed Blueberry Omelette

MY SATURDAY MORNING STANDBY – whether at home or out at a café – is a savoury omelette with parmesan and herbs, balanced by a tall glass of freshly squeezed orange juice. For something a little different (yet equally delicious), try this sweet take on the breakfast classic. It's light, fluffy and punctuated by juicy bursts of antioxidant-rich blueberries. A definite keeper.

## INGREDIENTS

125g punnet fresh blueberries
1 tbs water
2 eggs, separated
2 tbs Greek yogurt or coconut milk
½ tsp cinnamon
¼ tsp sea salt
1 tbs butter or coconut oil

## METHOD

1. Place a medium frying pan over medium-high heat. Add the blueberries and 1 tablespoon of water and cook for 5 minutes, until the blueberries have softened and are just beginning to release their juices. Transfer to a small bowl and set aside. Wipe the frying pan clean.

2. Whisk the egg yolks, yogurt or coconut milk, cinnamon and sea salt in a small bowl to combine. In a separate bowl, whisk the egg whites to stiff peaks. Carefully fold the egg whites through the yolk mixture.

3. Melt the butter or coconut oil in your frying pan over medium heat. Pour in the egg mixture and cook for 4–5 minutes, until almost set on top. Spoon half the blueberries onto one side of the omelette and carefully fold the omelette in half to enclose. Cook for a further 1–2 minutes, slide onto a plate and serve with the remaining blueberries.

Serves 1.

Don't Quit Sugar

# Mexican Egg Skillet

HERE'S A MEXICAN TWIST on the increasingly popular Middle Eastern shakshuka, or tomato-baked eggs. To make it extra special, serve with a bowl of fresh guacamole and some pure corn tortillas (if you can find them) in place of the sourdough.

## INGREDIENTS

1 tbs coconut oil or butter
1 small red onion, finely chopped
1 red capsicum, finely chopped
1 green capsicum, finely chopped
2 large tomatoes, seeds removed
   and finely chopped
2 garlic cloves, crushed
¾ cup (200g) tinned diced tomatoes
1 medium ear of corn, husk removed
4 large eggs
coriander leaves and finely sliced red
   onion, to garnish
toasted sourdough bread, to serve
1 lime, cut into wedges

## METHOD

1. Preheat the oven to 200°C.

2. Melt the coconut oil or butter in a large ovenproof frying pan over medium-high heat. Add the onion and capsicums; sauté for 2–3 minutes, until softened. Add the fresh tomato and garlic; continue to sauté, stirring occasionally, for 2–3 minutes more. Add the tinned tomatoes and season to taste with sea salt and pepper.

3. Use a sharp knife to remove the corn kernels from the cob (slice as close to the cob as possible so that some kernels remain clumped together). Add the corn kernels to the tomato mixture.

4. Make four indentations in the top of the mixture and crack an egg into each. Season each egg with salt and pepper. Bake for 10–15 minutes, until the egg whites are set but the yolks are still runny.

5. Scatter with coriander and sliced red onion and serve with toasted sourdough and lime wedges.

Serves 2.

# Melon with Passionfruit Syrup and Whipped Ricotta

WHIPPED RICOTTA IS REMINISCENT of a cannoli filling, yet is lighter and perfectly suited to breakfast. Here, it pairs beautifully with melons and passionfruit, but would work equally well with any fruit.

## INGREDIENTS

½ large rockmelon
½ large honeydew melon

Passionfruit syrup
½ cup passionfruit pulp
   (from approx. 8 passionfruit)
1 tsp raw honey
¼ cup water
juice of ½ lime
1 tbs finely shredded mint leaves

Whipped ricotta
2 cups ricotta cheese
½ cup milk
1 tbs raw honey
½ tsp vanilla extract

## METHOD

1. To make the passionfruit syrup, combine all ingredients in a small saucepan over medium heat. Bring to a boil, reduce the heat to medium-low and simmer for 10 minutes or until the mixture becomes syrupy. Set aside to cool.

2. Peel and deseed the rockmelon and honeydew melon halves. Slice lengthways into long, thin crescents.

3. With a whisk or electric beaters, beat together the ricotta, milk, honey and vanilla until light and fluffy.

4. Arrange the melon on plates, drizzle with syrup and serve with whipped ricotta.

Serves 4.

Don't Quit Sugar

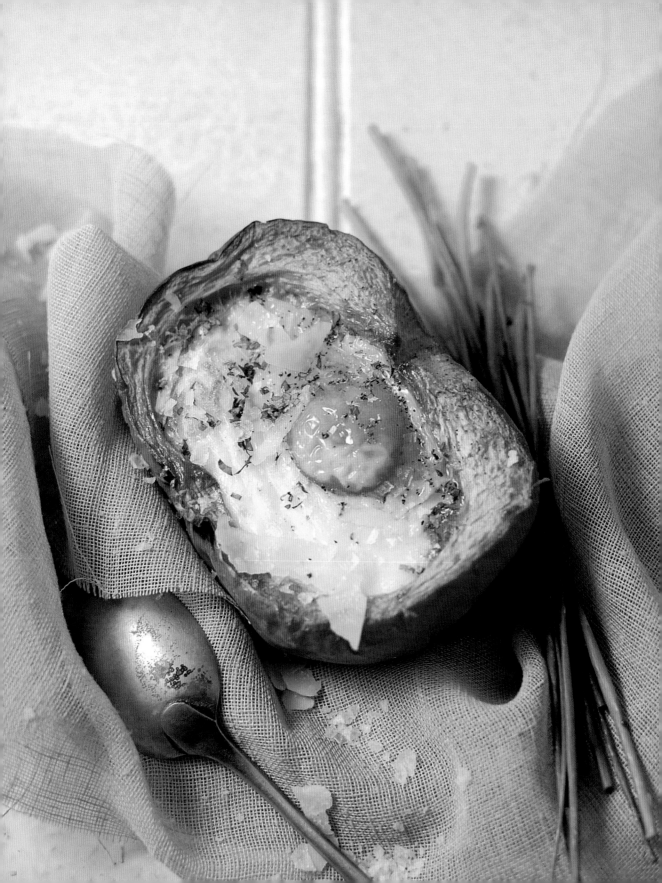

# Pumpkin Baked Eggs

THIS IS SUCH A SIMPLE YET SPECIAL BREAKFAST IDEA. Look for heirloom varieties of pumpkin at your greengrocer or local farmers' market. If pumpkins aren't available, you could easily substitute baked and hollowed-out sweet potatoes or large white potatoes.

INGREDIENTS

2 small pumpkins
1 tbs butter or coconut oil, melted
2 tbs finely grated parmesan
4 eggs
sea salt and freshly ground black
  pepper
1 tbs finely chopped herbs (thyme,
  sage, parsley and chives all work
  wonderfully)

METHOD

1. Preheat the oven to 200°C. Cut each pumpkin in half vertically and scoop out the seeds. Place each pumpkin half, cut side up, on a tray lined with baking paper. Drizzle with butter or coconut oil and bake for 20–30 minutes, until tender. (When the pumpkins are ready, a small knife should pass through the flesh easily.) Remove from the oven and allow to cool slightly.

2. Scatter half the parmesan into the base of each pumpkin half. Crack an egg into each and season with salt and pepper. Sprinkle with herbs and the remaining parmesan. Return to the oven for 10–15 minutes, until the egg whites are set but the yolks are still soft. Serve immediately.

Serves 2.

To save time, bake the pumpkins the night before. In the morning, simply fill them with the parmesan, eggs and herbs, and bake until the eggs are set.

# Warm Maple-Apple Bircher

OATS DON'T CONTAIN GLUTEN, however most commercial varieties are grown in fields alongside wheat, barley and rye and/or are processed in facilities that also process these gluten-containing grains. If you're gluten intolerant, it's important to source uncontaminated, gluten-free rolled oats. Soaking the oats overnight increases their digestibility.

## INGREDIENTS

1 cup rolled oats
2 tbs sultanas
1 cup (250ml) milk
1 cup (250g) Greek yogurt, plus
    extra to serve
1 tbs butter
4 Granny Smith apples, peeled,
    cored and chopped
1 tbs maple syrup
2 tsp cinnamon
2 tbs water

Apple Chips
2 apples

## METHOD

You'll need to begin this recipe the night before.

1. Combine the oats, sultanas, milk and yogurt in a large bowl. Cover and refrigerate overnight.

2. Melt the butter in a large saucepan over medium heat. Add the apples, maple syrup, cinnamon and water. Cover and cook for 15–20 minutes, stirring occasionally, until the apples are very tender.

3. Carefully fold 1 cup of the hot apples into the soaked oats to create a ripple effect. Divide between bowls and top with extra Greek yogurt, cooked apples and apple chips.

Apple Chips

1. Preheat the oven to 110°C. Line a large baking tray with baking paper.
2. Slice the apples as thinly as you can (a mandolin is ideal) and arrange, in a single layer, on the baking tray. Bake for 1 hour, flip the chips over (they'll be quite soft at this stage) and then bake for another hour. Allow the chips to cool completely in the oven. Store in an airtight container.

Serves 2.

Don't Quit Sugar

# Banana Split in a Jar

A HEALTHY MAKEOVER OF THIS DESSERT CLASSIC? Yes, please! As well as being a wonderful breakfast option, this could easily work as a mid-afternoon snack or as an entirely guilt-free after-dinner treat.

## INGREDIENTS

4 medium ripe bananas
2 cups (500g) Greek yogurt
2 tbs coconut flakes, to serve

Chocolate sauce
¼ cup cocoa powder
¼ cup maple syrup
2 tbs coconut oil, melted

Crushed strawberries
250g strawberries, diced
1 tsp honey
¼ cup water

## METHOD

1. For the chocolate sauce, combine all ingredients in a small bowl and stir until smooth.

2. For the crushed strawberries, combine all ingredients in a small saucepan over medium heat. Cook for 8–10 minutes, stirring occasionally, until the strawberries have softened and begin to release their juices. Crush with a fork to a rough puree and set aside to cool.

3. In a medium bowl, mash 2 bananas with a fork. Stir through the Greek yogurt to create a ripple effect.

4. Slice the remaining 2 bananas.

5. Divide the sliced bananas, stawberries and yogurt between four 1-cup capacity jars or glasses. Top with a drizzle of the chocolate sauce and a spoonful of coconut flakes.

Serves 4.

Store any leftover strawberries in the refrigerator; spoon over ice cream or yogurt, or use as a filling for a sweet omelette.

# LIGHT MEALS

Eating at regular intervals throughout the day will keep stress hormones low and blood sugar balanced.

The following light meals will provide sustained energy without weighing you down. Serve for lunch, as a snack, or even as appetisers to a multi-course dinner.

# Seared Beef Fillet with Figs, Parmesan and Rocket

PLUMP, JAMMY, PERFECTLY RIPE FIGS – classically referred to as the 'food of the gods' – are an absolute treat. In this simple Italian-inspired salad, their sweetness contrasts beautifully with savoury rare-cooked beef, peppery rocket and sharp parmesan.

## INGREDIENTS

2 tbs sea salt flakes
2 tbs freshly ground black pepper
500g piece top quality beef eye fillet
100g baby rocket leaves
6 ripe figs, sliced lengthways
2 spring onions, finely sliced
50g shaved parmesan
sea salt and freshly ground black
    pepper, to season
1 tbs extra virgin olive oil
1 tbs balsamic vinegar

## METHOD

1. Preheat a barbecue or heavy-bottomed frying pan over medium-high heat.

2. Combine the salt and pepper on a large plate then roll the beef fillet in the mixture to form an even crust.

3. Dry-sear the seasoned meat for 5 minutes on each side.

4. Reduce the heat to medium-low and continue cooking the beef, turning often, for an additional 10–15 minutes (for medium-rare). Transfer to a plate, cover with foil and allow to rest for 10–15 minutes.

5. Arrange the rocket on a large serving platter and scatter with the figs, spring onion and shaved parmesan. Season with salt and pepper.

6. Using a sharp knife, slice the beef as thinly as you can then drape the slices over and around the salad.

7. To finish, whisk together the olive oil and balsamic vinegar; drizzle over the salad.

Serves 4.

Don't Quit Sugar

# Roasted Beetroot with Orange Zest and Labneh

LABNEH IS A MIDDLE EASTERN YOGURT CHEESE simply made by straining yogurt to remove its whey component. The end result is thick, creamy, high in protein and perfect for adding to salads or smearing on quality sourdough. This salad – sweet beetroot, smooth labneh, fresh herbs and notes of orange – travels well, and so is a great take-to-work option.

## INGREDIENTS

1kg Greek yogurt

1 tsp sea salt

8 medium–large beetroot, stems removed and scrubbed clean (a mix of purple and yellow or pink beetroot is ideal)

1 tbs extra virgin olive oil

1 tsp apple cider vinegar

1 tsp raw honey

grated zest and juice of 1 small orange

½ small red onion, finely sliced

½ cup mixed fresh herbs (fennel fronds, parsley, thyme or chervil are all great)

## METHOD

You'll need to begin this recipe 2 days in advance.

1. To make the labneh, combine the yogurt with sea salt. Spoon into a paper towel–lined sieve set over a bowl. Cover with more paper towels and weigh down with a plate. Refrigerate and allow the yogurt to drain for 2 days.

2. When ready, remove the drained yogurt from the sieve and roll into small balls.

3. Preheat the oven to 200°C.

4. Wrap the beets individually in foil and place them on a baking tray. Roast for 45 minutes to 1 hour, until tender. To test, pierce the largest beet with a knife. If it enters easily, it's ready.

5. Allow the beets to cool, then peel with a paring knife (it's a good idea to wear gloves and to cover your chopping board with baking paper to prevent staining). Cut each beet into rough wedges.

6. In a small bowl, whisk together the olive oil, vinegar, honey, 1 teaspoon orange zest and 1 tablespoon orange juice.

7. Arrange the beets on a serving platter, scatter with red onion, herbs and labneh and drizzle over the dressing.

Serves 2–4 (depending on whether it is eaten for lunch or as an appetiser or side dish).

# Baked Ratatouille with Goat's Cheese

THIS IS SUCH A BEAUTIFUL WAY TO PREPARE AND PRESENT VEGETABLES (beyond some careful slicing, it really demands very little time or effort). Goat's cheese and sourdough are the perfect accompaniments, providing protein, fat-soluble vitamins and easily-digestible sugars.

## INGREDIENTS

2 tsp butter
1 small red onion, finely diced
1 clove garlic, crushed
1 small red capsicum, finely diced
2 cups (500ml) tomato passata
sea salt and freshly ground black
    pepper
2 medium zucchini
3 yellow (pattypan) squashes
2 long Japanese eggplants
4 roma tomatoes
5 sprigs fresh thyme
soft goat's cheese, to serve
sourdough bread, to serve

## METHOD

1. Melt the butter in a large saucepan over medium-low heat.

2. Sauté the onion, garlic and capsicum until softened, about 10–15 minutes.

3. Add the passata and season generously with salt and pepper. Pour the sauce into a round 25–30cm diameter casserole dish.

4. Slice the zucchini, squash, eggplants and tomatoes into even 5mm rounds, using a mandolin or very sharp knife. Arrange the vegetable slices, alternating and overlapping slightly, in a concentric pattern on top of the tomato sauce mixture. Season with salt and pepper and scatter with thyme. Cover with a round of baking paper cut to fit the top of the casserole dish.

5. Bake for 45 minutes to an hour, until the vegetables are tender and the sauce is bubbling.

6. Serve with fresh sourdough bread and goat's cheese.

Serves 4.

Don't Quit Sugar

# Prawn, Watermelon and Feta Salad

SHELLFISH ARE PARTICULARLY HIGH IN SELENIUM, necessary for the conversion of thyroid hormone T4 to (active) thyroid hormone T3. In this classic combination, the sweet prawns and juicy watermelon are offset by salty feta and sharp red onion. A delicious starter to a summer seafood lunch.

## INGREDIENTS

1 small seedless watermelon
16 cooked medium king prawns, peeled (tails left intact), deveined
2 small Lebanese cucumbers, peeled and sliced into half moons
½ small red onion, finely sliced
150g feta cheese, coarsely crumbled
½ cup packed fresh mint leaves, roughly chopped
1 tbs lemon juice
1 tbs extra virgin olive oil
¼ tsp freshly ground black pepper

## METHOD

1. Place the watermelon on its side. Using a large sharp knife, cut four 2cm-thick slices. Lay each slice flat on your chopping board and, using a smaller knife, remove the rind to create four discs of watermelon flesh.

2. In a large bowl, combine the prawns, cucumber, onion, feta and mint. Drizzle with the lemon juice and olive oil, season with pepper and toss gently.

3. To serve, arrange the watermelon discs on individual plates and top with a generous pile of the salad.

Serves 4.

To make this salad work-lunch friendly, simply chop the watermelon into cubes and pack into a container with the remaining ingredients.

# Chilli Lime Tuna Skewers with Shaved Pineapple

PINEAPPLE CONTAINS THE ENZYME BROMELAIN, which assists in protein digestion. The body is less able to assimilate proteins from raw or rare-cooked fish and meat; eating rare tuna alongside pineapple will therefore maximise its digestion.

## INGREDIENTS

8 small wooden cocktail skewers
500g sashimi-quality tuna fillet
zest of 1 lime
1 garlic clove, crushed
1 long red chilli, seeds removed,
  finely chopped
½ tsp sea salt flakes
¼ tsp freshly ground black pepper
coconut oil, for brushing
lime halves, to serve

### Shaved pineapple salad

½ small pineapple
½ cup packed mint leaves, finely
  chopped
1 long red chilli, seeds removed,
  finely chopped
½ small red onion, finely chopped
juice of ½ lime

## METHOD

1. Submerge the wooden skewers in a small bowl of water for 20 minutes.

2. Using a sharp knife, cut the tuna into 3cm cubes. In a non-reactive bowl (such as one of stainless steel or glass), combine the tuna with the lime zest, garlic, chilli, salt and pepper. Set aside to marinate for 10–20 minutes.

3. Peel the pineapple and remove the core. Slice very thinly crossways. Toss with the mint, chilli, onion and lime juice and divide between serving plates.

4. Preheat a barbecue or grill pan on medium-high heat and brush lightly with coconut oil. Thread 2–3 cubes of tuna onto each skewer. Grill for 30–60 seconds on each side, until browned but still rare in the centre. Serve alongside the shaved pineapple with extra lime halves for squeezing.

Serves 4.

Don't Quit Sugar

# Snapper Ceviche with Mango and Coconut

CEVICHE IS A TRADITIONAL CENTRAL AND SOUTH AMERICAN DISH of raw fish 'cooked' in citrus juice. Here, I lean towards Caribbean flavours with the use of fresh mango, coriander and coconut.

## INGREDIENTS

500g fresh snapper fillets, skinned and boned
½ cup freshly squeezed lime juice
½ small red onion, finely chopped
1 Lebanese cucumber, peeled, seeded and finely chopped
1 medium tomato, seeds removed, finely chopped
½ cup finely chopped coriander leaves
sea salt and freshly ground black pepper
1 firm mango, flesh diced into 1cm cubes
270ml can coconut milk

## METHOD

1. Using a sharp knife, chop the fish as finely as you can. Place in a shallow dish and pour over the lime juice. Allow to sit for 10 minutes, until the fish has turned opaque. Drain, discarding the liquid.

2. Combine the fish with the onion, cucumber, tomato and coriander and toss to mix. Season to taste with sea salt and black pepper. Add the mango and toss gently to incorporate.

3. Divide between serving glasses and drizzle with coconut milk.

Serves 4.

If you're keen to impress, serve the ceviche with homemade sweet potato chips. Use a mandolin slicer to slice a large sweet potato as thinly as possible (1–2mm). Heat coconut oil in a large pot to 160°C and deep-fry the slices in batches until golden and crisp. Drain on paper towel.

# Eggplant, Fig and Mozzarella Sandwiches

THIS IS A HEALTHY TAKE ON THE ITALIAN COMFORT FOOD *mozzarella in carrozza*, essentially a fried mozzarella sandwich. Lightly crumbed slices of eggplant substitute for bread and are filled with creamy cheese, sweet figs and fragrant basil. Eat these sandwiches piping hot; you want the mozzarella oozing and the breadcrumbs crispy.

## INGREDIENTS

4 slices day-old sourdough bread, torn
3 eggs
sea salt and freshly ground black pepper
2 medium eggplants, sliced into 1cm rounds
2 tbs butter, melted
100g buffalo mozzarella, thinly sliced
4 ripe figs, sliced
½ bunch basil, leaves picked

## METHOD

1. Preheat the oven to 180°C and line two large baking trays with baking paper.

2. Using a food processor, pulse the bread to breadcrumbs and tip into a shallow bowl. Beat the eggs in a separate shallow bowl and season with sea salt and black pepper.

3. One at a time, dip the eggplant slices into the beaten eggs and then into the breadcrumbs to coat. Arrange in a single layer on the prepared baking trays and drizzle with the melted butter. Bake for 15–20 minutes, until golden brown and soft. Remove from the oven and allow to cool slightly.

4. Layer a slice of mozzarella, a slice of fig and one large or two small basil leaves onto half of the eggplant slices. Sandwich with the remaining eggplant slices. Return to the oven for 5–10 minutes, until the mozzarella is melted. Serve immediately.

Serves 4.

Don't Quit Sugar

# Chicken and Rice Dumpling Soup

ON A BLUSTERY WINTER'S DAY, nothing beats a comforting bowl of old-fashioned chicken soup. In this recipe, the chicken and rice dumplings add heartiness and provide natural sugars and extra protein. Be sure to use homemade chicken stock for maximum flavour and for its powerful anti-inflammatory properties.

## INGREDIENTS

For the broth

2 tbs butter
2 large leeks, halved, rinsed and finely sliced
2 large carrots, finely diced
4 large celery stalks, finely diced
2 garlic cloves, crushed
8 cups (2L) homemade chicken stock (recipe page 145)
sea salt and freshly ground black pepper

For the dumplings

750g chicken mince
½ cup uncooked long grain white rice, rinsed
1 egg, beaten
1 garlic clove, crushed
2 lbs finely chopped flat-leaf parsley, or 1 tsp dried parsley
1 tsp sea salt
½ tsp freshly ground black pepper
¼ cup chopped fresh dill, to serve

## METHOD

1. For the broth, melt the butter in a large pot over medium heat. Add the leek, carrot and celery and cook, stirring often, for 8–10 minutes, until the vegetables are softened. Add the garlic and cook for a further 2 minutes. Add the chicken stock and bring to a boil. Reduce to a simmer and season to taste with sea salt and black pepper.

2. For the dumplings, combine all ingredients in a large bowl and use your hands to mix thoroughly. Form the mixture into golf ball–sized balls and gently lower them into the broth. Simmer for 30–40 minutes, until the rice is cooked through and the vegetables are tender. Adjust the seasoning if necessary and ladle into serving bowls. Garnish with dill.

Serves 4.

The dumplings freeze incredibly well. Make a double batch and freeze half – raw or cooked – spaced well apart in a freezerproof container, so that they are ready to be simmered in steaming broth at a moment's notice.

# Spring Vegetable Casserole with Eggs

THIS DISH IS PERFECT FOR ENTERTAINING and works equally well for breakfast, lunch or dinner. For ease, cook the vegetables before your guests arrive; then, 15 minutes before you're ready to eat, simply add the eggs and bake.

## INGREDIENTS

500g baby (chat) potatoes, halved

1 tbs butter

4 leeks, thinly sliced

2 bunches asparagus, ends trimmed, stalks halved lengthways if they are thick

1 cup frozen peas

½ cup vegetable stock

1 tbs fresh thyme leaves

sea salt and freshly ground black pepper

4 eggs

shaved parmesan, to serve

## METHOD

1. Preheat the oven to 200°C.

2. Place the potatoes in a large saucepan and cover with cold water. Add a generous pinch of sea salt and bring to the boil over medium-high heat. Reduce the heat to medium and simmer for 5–10 minutes, until the potatoes are just tender. Drain and set aside.

3. Melt the butter in a large frying pan over medium heat. Add the sliced leeks and sauté for 5–10 minutes until softened. Add the potatoes, asparagus, peas, stock and thyme to the pan, tossing to combine. Season generously with sea salt and black pepper.

4. Transfer the vegetables to a large casserole dish. Make four indentations in the top of the mixture and crack an egg into each. Bake for 10–15 minutes, until the egg whites are set but the yolks are still runny. Serve immediately with a sprinkling of shaved parmesan.

Serves 4.

Don't Quit Sugar

# Grilled Haloumi with Fresh Cherries and Basil

HALOUMI AND CHERRIES AREN'T A TRADITIONAL PAIRING by any means, but served this way they just make so much sense. The salty creaminess of the haloumi works beautifully with the sharp/sweet juiciness of the cherries and the punch of red onion and basil.

## INGREDIENTS

2 cups cherries, pitted and chopped

1 eschalot (or ¼ small red onion), finely chopped

½ small green capsicum, finely chopped

2 tbs finely sliced fresh basil leaves

1 tsp balsamic vinegar

sea salt and freshly ground black pepper

melted coconut oil, for brushing

300g haloumi cheese, sliced crossways into 1cm-thick rectangles

## METHOD

1. In a small bowl, combine the chopped cherries, eschalot, capsicum, basil and balsamic vinegar. Season to taste with sea salt and black pepper. Set aside.

2. Heat a chargrill or heavy-bottomed frying pan over medium-high heat and brush with melted coconut oil. Grill the haloumi slices for 1–2 minutes each side, until slightly charred and beginning to melt. Transfer to plates and serve topped with the cherry salsa.

Serves 2–4 (depending on whether it is served as an appetiser or lunch).

# MAINS

A macronutrient-balanced dinner paves the way for a restful night's sleep.

Natural sugars are easy (and delicious) to incorporate – think roasted or mashed root vegetables and ripe, tropical fruits in fragrant Asian- and Mediterranean-style salads.

Sources of protein will depend on your personal preferences; in the following recipes, feel free to substitute lamb for beef or chicken for fish.

# Slow-Roast Lamb Shoulder with Pomegranate Molasses and Turkish Spoon Salad

LAMB LENDS ITSELF WONDERFULLY to Moroccan and Middle Eastern flavours. Perfect for entertaining is this slow-roast shoulder with sweet/tart pomegranate and a vibrant chopped salad. Pomegranate molasses is available at delis and specialty food stores.

## INGREDIENTS

For the lamb
1.6–1.8kg shoulder of lamb, bone in
½ cup pomegranate molasses
2 tbs raw honey
4 cloves garlic, crushed
1 tsp ground cumin
juice of 3 lemons
2 tsp sea salt flakes
1 tsp freshly ground black pepper

Spoon salad
4 Lebanese cucumbers, peeled, seeds removed, finely chopped
4 large ripe tomatoes, seeds removed, finely chopped
1 red capsicum, finely chopped
1 green capsicum, finely chopped
1 small red onion, finely diced
1 cup pomegranate seeds (2–3 pomegranates)
1 cup finely chopped mint
1 cup finely chopped flat-leaf parsley

Dressing
2 tbs extra virgin olive oil
1 tbs lemon juice
1 tbs pomegranate molasses
1 tsp sumac
sea salt and freshly ground black pepper
Greek yogurt, to serve

## METHOD

1. Pierce the lamb all over and cut a few deep slits with a small sharp knife. Place in a heavy-bottomed casserole dish or in a roasting tin. Add the pomegranate molasses, honey, garlic, cumin, lemon juice and seasoning and massage into the lamb. Refrigerate for 8 hours or overnight.

2. Preheat the oven to 140°C. If using a casserole dish, cover with its lid; if using a roasting tray, tent it with foil to cover. Roast the lamb for 3–4 hours, occasionally basting it with its juices, until the meat is very tender.

3. Combine all the salad ingredients in a large bowl. For the dressing, whisk together the olive oil, lemon juice, pomegranate molasses and sumac, and season to taste. Pour over the salad and toss to combine.

4. Slice the lamb and serve with the salad and Greek yogurt.

Serves 4–6.

# Lamb Shank Tagine
# with Dates and Prunes

A DEFINITE WINTER WARMER, this recipe marries heady Moroccan spices, sweet dried fruit and fork-meltingly tender shank meat. Like all stews, the flavour will only improve with time, so make it on the weekend to enjoy during the week.

## INGREDIENTS

2 tbs coconut oil

4 x 375g lamb shanks

1 large brown onion, halved and thinly sliced

3 cloves garlic, crushed

2 tsp each ground cumin, coriander, paprika and cinnamon

1 tsp ground ginger

¼ cup tomato paste

4 cups (1L) homemade beef stock (broth recipe page 145)

pinch saffron threads

2 tsp sea salt flakes

1 tsp freshly ground black pepper

1 cup each pitted dates and prunes

400g sweet potato, peeled and chopped into 4cm chunks

½ cup packed coriander leaves, roughly chopped

½ cup packed flat-leaf parsley leaves, roughly chopped

## METHOD

1. Preheat oven to 150°C.

2. In a large heavy-based or cast-iron pot, melt 1 tablespoon of the coconut oil over medium-high heat. Sear the lamb shanks, in two batches if necessary, turning to brown all over. Transfer to a plate and set aside.

3. In the same pot, melt the remaining tablespoon of coconut oil. Reduce the heat to medium and sauté the onion for 5–10 minutes, until softened. Add the garlic and spices and cook, stirring, for 2–3 minutes until fragrant. Add the tomato paste, beef stock, saffron, salt, pepper, prunes and dates and stir to combine. Finally, add the sweet potato and lamb shanks, ensuring that both are properly submerged in liquid (add a little water if necessary).

4. Bring to a boil, cover with a tight-fitting lid and transfer to the oven. Bake for 2–2½ hours, until the lamb is meltingly tender and the sauce has thickened. Serve scattered with coriander and parsley.

Serves 4.

Don't Quit Sugar

# Barbecued Whole Snapper with Papaya Salsa

WHEN BUYING A WHOLE FISH, look for clear eyes, shiny skin and a smell of the sea, all of which indicate freshness. Ask your fishmonger to gut, clean and scale it for you.

## INGREDIENTS

1.5–2kg whole snapper, gutted and scaled
2 limes, thinly sliced (with skin), plus extra wedges to serve
5cm piece of ginger, sliced
2 garlic cloves, sliced
½ small bunch coriander
sea salt and freshly ground black pepper

### Papaya salsa

2 small (or 1 large) papayas, peeled, seeds removed, chopped into 1.5cm cubes
½ red onion, finely chopped
¼ cup finely chopped coriander leaves (use the other half of the bunch from the fish)
2 red chillies, seeds removed, finely chopped
juice of 1 lime

## METHOD

1. Preheat a barbecue to medium-high. Rinse the fish, inside and out, under cold running water and then pat dry with paper towels.

2. Using a sharp knife, cut three 1cm-deep slashes in the thickest part of each side of the fish (this will help it cook evenly).

3. Roll out a piece of foil large enough to envelop the fish and place a piece of baking paper of the same size on top of the foil. Lay the fish in the centre of the baking paper. Fill the fish cavity with the lime slices, ginger, garlic and coriander and season the whole fish with salt and pepper. Fold up the baking paper and foil to enclose the fish, scrunching it to secure.

4. Barbecue the fish, with the hood down, for 25–35 minutes, or until the flesh is opaque and flakes easily with a fork.

5. Meanwhile, for the salsa, place all ingredients in a medium bowl and toss to combine. Season with salt and pepper to taste.

6. Serve the fish on a large platter, topped with the salsa and extra lime wedges.

Serves 4.

If you don't have a barbecue, you can cook the fish in the oven. Bake for 25–35 minutes at 180°C or until the flesh flakes easily with a fork.

# Vietnamese Grilled Chicken with Lychee Salad

LIGHT, FRAGRANT AND PACKED WITH FLAVOUR, this salad epitomises summer eating. It's perhaps my favourite illustration of how to combine tropical fruits with protein to create a perfectly balanced meal.

## INGREDIENTS

¼ cup rice vinegar
¼ cup lime juice
¼ cup raw honey or palm sugar
2 tbs fish sauce
2 tbs soy sauce or tamari
3 cloves garlic, roughly chopped
2 eschalots, roughly chopped
1 stalk lemongrass, finely sliced
thumb-sized knob of ginger, peeled
   and roughly chopped
750g skinless chicken thigh fillets

### Salad

1 large telegraph cucumber, halved
   lengthways and thinly sliced
2 eschalots, thinly sliced
2 spring onions, white and green
   parts thinly sliced on a diagonal
1 cup packed mint leaves
1 cup packed coriander leaves
1 cup bean sprouts
20 fresh lychees, peeled and seeds
   removed
½ cup dried coconut flakes, plus
   extra to serve

## METHOD

1. In a small bowl or jug, whisk together the rice vinegar, lime juice, honey or palm sugar, fish sauce and soy sauce or tamari.

2. Using a food processor or a mortar and pestle, grind the garlic, eschalots, lemongrass and ginger to a rough paste. Stir in half the rice vinegar mixture to form a marinade (reserve the remaining half for the salad dressing).

3. Place the chicken thighs in a non-reactive bowl; pour over the marinade and mix to coat evenly. Cover and refrigerate for at least 2 hours or overnight.

4. Preheat a barbecue or grill pan to high heat. Remove the chicken thighs from the marinade, shaking off any excess. Grill for 5–8 minutes on each side, until slightly charred and cooked through.

5. For the salad, combine ingredients in a large bowl. Pour over the reserved rice vinegar mixture and toss to combine.

6. Serve the salad topped with the chicken thighs and a sprinkling of coconut flakes.

Serves 4.

Don't Quit Sugar

# Simple Baked Fish and Root Vegetables

THIS IS AN EXTREMELY VERSATILE (and entirely undemanding) midweek dinner option. Consider the listed vegetables as suggestions only – really, any seasonal root vegetables will work. Similarly, if you can't find swordfish, tuna steaks, blue-eye, John Dory and snapper are all beautiful alternatives.

## INGREDIENTS

4 x 200g thick swordfish fillets
sea salt and freshly ground black pepper
1 lemon, thinly sliced
8–10 sprigs thyme
3 tbs coconut oil, melted
2 tbs raw honey
2 bunches baby carrots (about 12), washed and stems trimmed
2 bunches beetroot (about 6), washed and cut into wedges
12 baby (chat) potatoes, halved
2 large fennel bulbs, trimmed and cut into wedges
6 garlic cloves, whole and unpeeled
lemon wedges, to serve

## METHOD

1. Preheat the oven to 180°C. Line two large roasting trays with baking paper.

2. Lay the fish fillets in one roasting tray and season with sea salt and black pepper. Cover each fillet with 2–3 slices of lemon and scatter with half the thyme sprigs. Drizzle with 1 tablespoon of the melted coconut oil and 1 tablespoon of honey. Set aside.

3. Arrange the carrots, beetroot, potatoes, fennel and garlic in a single layer in the second roasting tray. Drizzle with the remaining 2 tablespoons of coconut oil and tablespoon of honey and toss gently to coat. Season with sea salt and black pepper and scatter with the remaining thyme sprigs. Bake for 35–40 minutes, until the vegetables are golden and almost tender.

4. Add the tray of fish to the oven and cook for an additional 12–15 minutes, or until the fish flakes easily with a fork and the vegetables are cooked through. Serve with lemon wedges.

Serves 4.

# Mexican Mince-Stuffed Sweet Potatoes

AN EXTREMELY EASY (and crowd-pleasing) weeknight dinner. Additional toppings are up to you; I prefer Greek yogurt and a chunky guacamole, though roasted corn kernels or a fresh tomato and coriander salsa would each be scrumptious.

## INGREDIENTS

4 medium sweet potatoes, scrubbed
1 tbs coconut oil
1 large red onion, finely chopped
1 large red capsicum, finely chopped
500g beef mince
2 cloves garlic, crushed
2 tsp ground cumin
1 tsp ground coriander
1 tsp paprika
½ tsp cayenne pepper (optional)
1 tsp dried oregano
sea salt and freshly ground black
    pepper
2 tbs tomato paste
1 cup tomato passata
1 cup water
1 avocado, halved and stoned
juice of ½ lime
200g Greek yogurt, to serve
    (optional)
small bunch coriander, leaves
    picked, to serve

## METHOD

1. Preheat the oven to 200°C. Place the whole sweet potatoes on a lined baking tray, and bake for 45 minutes to an hour, until soft.

2. Meanwhile, melt the coconut oil in a large frying pan over medium-high heat. Sauté the onion and capsicum for 5–10 minutes until softened. Add the beef mince and cook, breaking up with a spoon, until browned. Stir in the garlic, spices and oregano and cook for an additional 5 minutes, until fragrant. Season generously with salt and pepper and add the tomato paste, passata and water. Bring to a boil, reduce the heat to low and simmer gently until the sweet potatoes are ready.

3. In a small bowl, mash together the avocado flesh, lime juice and a pinch of sea salt.

4. To serve, cut a deep pocket along the top of each sweet potato and fill with the mince mixture. Top with a spoonful each of avocado and yogurt and scatter with coriander.

Serves 4.

Don't Quit Sugar

# Spiced Chicken with Apricots and Olives

IF YOU LIKE YOUR CHICKEN FLAVOUR-PACKED, this recipe is a must to try. The secret is in the marinade: it infuses the chicken with sweetness and spice and guarantees a most tender roasting. Ensure you use an organic, free-range chook; most butchers will happily chop it up for you.

## INGREDIENTS

1.8–2kg whole chicken, cut into 8 pieces
12 ripe apricots, halved, stones removed
¼ cup fresh lemon juice
2 tbs raw honey
1 tsp ground cumin
1 tsp ground cinnamon
1 tsp smoked Spanish paprika
½–1 tsp chilli flakes (depending on how spicy you want it)
2 tsp sea salt
1 tsp freshly ground black pepper
1 large red onion, halved and finely sliced
1 cup green olives, halved
1 cup packed coriander leaves, roughly chopped, plus extra to serve
120g baby rocket
1 tbs extra virgin olive oil

## METHOD

1. Arrange the chicken pieces, skin side up, in a single layer in a large roasting dish.

2. Use a food processor or blender to process 4 apricots (8 halves) to a puree. Add the lemon juice, honey, cumin, cinnamon, paprika, chilli, sea salt and black pepper and pulse to combine. Pour the mixture over the chicken pieces and refrigerate for at least 4 hours or overnight.

3. Preheat the oven to 160°C.

4. Cover the roasting dish tightly with foil and bake for 1 hour.

5. Remove from the oven, discard the foil and add the red onion, olives, coriander leaves and remaining apricot halves. Use a large metal spoon to gently mix everything together, ensuring the chicken pieces remain skin side up. Increase the oven temperature to 200°C and bake for an additional 20–25 minutes, until the chicken is golden and the apricots are tender.

6. Serve straight from the roasting dish atop a pile of peppery rocket drizzled with olive oil.

Serves 4.

Don't Quit Sugar

# Open-Face Steak Sandwich with Quick Beetroot Relish

The quintessential Aussie classic is jazzed up with an orange-perfumed beetroot relish.

## INGREDIENTS

4 x 150g scotch fillet steaks
sea salt and freshly ground black
  pepper
2 tbs butter
1 large red onion, halved and finely
  sliced
4 thick slices quality sourdough
  bread, toasted
2 ripe tomatoes, thickly sliced
2 large handfuls rocket leaves

Beetroot relish

4 medium beetroots, peeled and
  finely chopped (you want about
  2 cups of chopped beetroot)
1 small red onion, finely chopped
½ cup freshly squeezed orange juice
1 tsp finely grated orange zest
1 tbs raw honey
2 tbs red wine vinegar or apple cider
  vinegar
1 tsp sea salt
½ tsp freshly ground black pepper

## METHOD

1. For the beetroot relish, combine all ingredients in a medium pot over medium-high heat. Bring to a boil, reduce the heat to medium and cook for 25–30 minutes, until the beetroot is soft and the mixture is thick and syrupy. Transfer to a small bowl or jar and allow to cool.

2. Season the steaks on both sides with sea salt and black pepper. Heat 1½ tablespoons of butter in a large frying pan over high heat. Add the steaks and cook for 2–3 minutes each side for medium or until cooked to your liking. Transfer to a plate to rest.

3. Heat the remaining butter in the same frying pan over medium-high heat. Add the onion and sauté until soft, 5–7 minutes. Remove from the heat.

4. Slice the steaks thinly crossways. To assemble the sandwiches, layer each slice of sourdough with the onions, tomato, steak slices, rocket and beetroot relish. Serve with extra beetroot relish to the side.

Serves 4.

# Spinach and Ricotta Gnocchi with Pumpkin Sauce and Roast Tomatoes

HERE, I REPLACE TRADITIONAL POTATO AND FLOUR GNOCCHI with pillowy balls of spinach and ricotta. High in protein, calcium and fat-soluble vitamins, these gnocchi are nicely balanced by the sucrose and starch in a velvety pumpkin puree.

## INGREDIENTS

300g frozen spinach, thawed
500g fresh ricotta, drained
⅓ cup finely grated parmesan,
   plus extra to serve
2 egg yolks, lightly beaten
sea salt and freshly ground black
   pepper
¼ cup fresh sage leaves
1 tbs butter, melted
300g vine-ripened cherry tomatoes

### Pumpkin puree
1 tbs butter
½ small brown onion, chopped
1 small garlic clove, crushed
500g butternut pumpkin, skin
   removed, diced into 2cm cubes
2 cups homemade chicken broth,
   vegetable broth or water

If you're time poor, prepare the gnocchi on the weekend so that they're ready to bake for a quick midweek dinner. Serve with a simple tomato sauce in place of the pumpkin puree and balance the meal with a piece of fruit for dessert.

## METHOD

1. Preheat the oven to 180°C. Line two baking trays with baking paper.

2. Gather the thawed spinach in a clean tea towel and squeeze to remove as much moisture as possible. Transfer to a chopping board and chop finely.

3. In a large bowl, combine the spinach, ricotta, parmesan and egg yolks. Season generously with salt and pepper and mix until smooth (no lumps should remain). Shape the mixture into small balls, place on a prepared baking tray, scatter with the sage leaves and drizzle with the melted butter. Place the cherry tomatoes on the second prepared baking tray. Bake the gnocchi and tomatoes for 20–25 minutes, until the tomatoes have softened and the gnocchi is golden.

4. Meanwhile, for the pumpkin puree, melt the butter over medium heat, using the spinach cooking pot. Add the onion and garlic and sauté until softened, about 5 minutes. Add the pumpkin and broth (or water) and bring to a boil. Reduce the heat to medium-low and cook for 15 minutes, or until the pumpkin is tender. Transfer the pumpkin and 1 cup of the cooking liquid to a blender and process until smooth. Add more of the cooking liquid, if necessary, to achieve a sauce-like consistency. Season to taste with salt and pepper.

5. To serve, ladle the pumpkin puree onto plates and top with the gnocchi and cherry tomatoes. Sprinkle with extra parmesan, if desired.

Serves 4.

Don't Quit Sugar

# Coconut Curry Soup with Rice Noodles and Eggs

THIS SOUP IS ONE OF MY ABSOLUTE FAVOURITES. Nourishing, gelatinous chicken broth deeply flavoured with Thai herbs and spices, slippery rice noodles, crunchy bean sprouts, the tang of lime and a nutrient-rich sunny omelette to finish. My mouth is watering already.

## INGREDIENTS

4 cups (1L) homemade chicken
   broth (see recipe page 145)
thumb-sized knob fresh ginger, finely
   grated
2 large garlic cloves, crushed
3 eschalots, finely sliced
4 kaffir lime leaves, finely sliced
1 stalk lemongrass, bruised with the
   back of a large knife and finely
   sliced
2 heaped tbs Thai curry powder
270ml coconut milk
100g dried rice noodles
1 tbs butter
4 eggs
sea salt and freshly ground black
   pepper
1 small bunch coriander, leaves
   picked
½ bunch Thai basil, leaves picked
½ bunch mint, leaves picked
1 cup bean sprouts
juice of 1 lime

## METHOD

1. In a large pot, bring the chicken broth, ginger, garlic, eschalots, lime leaves, lemongrass and curry powder to a simmer. Add the coconut milk and stir to combine.

2. Prepare the rice noodles according to packet instructions and divide between two serving bowls.

3. In your largest non-stick frying pan, melt half the butter over medium-low heat. Whisk 2 eggs in a small bowl, season with sea salt and black pepper, then pour into the pan, tilting the pan so that the eggs coat the base thinly and evenly. Cook until just set (2–3 minutes) and then slide the omelette out of the pan and onto a chopping board or large plate. Repeat with the remaining butter and eggs.

4. To serve, ladle the infused broth over the rice noodles. Garnish with the picked herbs and bean sprouts and add lime juice to taste. Top with the folded omelettes.

Serves 2.

For a vegetarian version, simply replace the chicken broth with homemade (or good-quality store-bought) vegetable broth.

As an alternative to the omelette, serve the soup topped with halved soft-boiled eggs.

# DESSERTS

After dinner most nights, I'll usually reach for a handful of berries and a few spoonfuls of Greek yogurt; it's simple, balanced and truly satisfying.

Dessert needn't be associated with guilt. The following recipes transform the most nourishing of ingredients – fruit, dairy, eggs, coconut, raw honey, plus a little dark chocolate – into a plethora of mouth-watering, blood-sugar-balancing and naturally sweet treats.

# Mango and Passionfruit Ricotta Cheesecake

THIS CHEESECAKE IS SO VIRTUOUS you could serve it for breakfast without guilt: calcium-packed Greek yogurt and ricotta, micronutrient-rich eggs and natural sugars from tropical mango, passionfruit and a little honey.

## INGREDIENTS

For the cheesecake
800g fresh ricotta cheese
250g (1 cup) Greek yogurt
5 large eggs, separated
½ cup raw honey
2 tsp vanilla extract
1½ cups diced mango flesh
   (from 2 large firm mangoes)
¼ tsp sea salt

For the topping
250g (1 cup) Greek yogurt
2 large, firm mangoes, peeled and
   sliced into thin strips
¾ cup fresh passionfruit pulp
   (10–12 passionfruit)

## METHOD

1. Preheat the oven to 160°C. Line a 20cm springform cake tin with baking paper.

2. For the cheesecake, blend the ricotta, yogurt, egg yolks, honey and vanilla in a food processor until very smooth. Transfer to a large bowl and stir through the chopped mango.

3. In a separate bowl, add the salt to the egg whites and beat until they form firm peaks.

4. Gently fold one-third of the egg whites into the ricotta mixture. Add the remaining egg whites and fold to combine.

5. Pour the mixture into the prepared tin and bake for 1 hour, or until golden and set.

6. Allow to cool in the oven (leave the oven door ajar) and then refrigerate until cold.

7. To serve, top the cheesecake with the yogurt and mango slices and drizzle with the passionfruit pulp.

Serves 8–10.

# Seriously Chocolate Cake

AS ITS NAME SUGGESTS, THIS CAKE IS VERY RICH; a small sliver is all that's needed to truly satisfy. It only contains a short list of ingredients, so it's important to source the best you can find – quality dark chocolate, organic butter and pastured eggs with healthy, sun-coloured yolks.

## INGREDIENTS

300g medjool dates, pitted and chopped into small pieces (approx 15 large dates)
½ cup orange juice
300g dark (70%) chocolate, chopped
150g butter, chopped
6 large eggs, separated
¼ cup cocoa powder
¼ tsp sea salt

## METHOD

1. Preheat oven to 160°C and line a 23cm diameter cake tin with baking paper.

2. Combine the dates and orange juice in a small saucepan. Simmer over medium heat until the dates have softened and have absorbed the orange juice. Mash with the back of a spoon to a rough puree.

3. Place the chocolate and butter in large heatproof bowl set over a pan of simmering water (don't let the bowl touch the water). Stir occasionally until melted and smooth. Remove the bowl from the heat and stir in the egg yolks, one at a time, followed by the date mixture. Sift over the cocoa powder and stir to combine.

4. In a separate bowl, beat the egg whites and salt to firm peaks. Thoroughly stir one-third of the egg whites into the chocolate mixture, then carefully fold in the remaining egg whites until no white streaks remain.

5. Pour the mixture into the prepared cake tin and bake for 40–45 minutes, until just set (the centre of the cake will still be quite moist).

Substitute the dates for another dried fruit – plump dried figs or prunes will each work beautifully.

Don't Quit Sugar

# The Simplest Mocha Mousse (Dairy-Free)

THERE SEEM TO BE INNUMERABLE VERSIONS OF 'WHOLE FOOD' CHOCOLATE MOUSSE – recipes based on avocado, coconut milk or protein powder, sweetened with dates, banana or (sugar-free) stevia. None (at least in my opinion) can surpass the flavour and texture of the original. *Real*, pared-back chocolate mousse – just egg yolks, egg whites and top-quality bitter chocolate – is deeply satisfying and incredibly nourishing\*. This recipe steps it up a notch with the addition of coffee. For a pure chocolate version, simply replace the espresso with water.

## INGREDIENTS

120g dark (70%) chocolate
¼ cup brewed espresso or
    strong coffee
4 eggs, separated
1 tbs maple syrup, optional
seasonal fruit, coconut flakes
    or cocoa powder, to serve

## METHOD

1. Combine the chocolate and espresso in a large heatproof bowl set over a pan of simmering water (don't let the bowl touch the water). Stir occasionally until the chocolate has melted and the mixture is smooth. Remove from the heat.

2. One at a time, whisk the egg yolks into the chocolate mixture. Stir in the maple syrup, if using.

3. In a separate bowl, beat the egg whites to firm peaks. Stir a quarter of the egg whites into the chocolate. Carefully fold in the remaining egg whites until no white streaks remain. Try to maintain as much air in the mixture as possible.

4. Divide the mousse between four serving cups and refrigerate for at least 2 hours. Serve with fruit, coconut flakes or dusted with cocoa powder.

Makes 4.

\*Eggs – easily assimilable protein, healthy saturated fat, vitamins A, B, D, E and K, calcium, zinc, selenium, hormone-building cholesterol.

Dark chocolate – magnesium, copper, zinc, manganese, healthy saturated cocoa fat.

# Coconut Crème Brûlée

THE USE OF COCONUT CREAM MAKES THIS RECIPE DAIRY-FREE but maintains the silky lusciousness of traditional crème brûlée. Coconut sugar, which is available from health food stores, has a unique, caramel-like complexity; if you can't find it, substitute palm sugar.

## INGREDIENTS

4 large egg yolks
¼ cup coconut sugar, plus
   1 tbs extra
400ml can coconut cream
fresh passionfruit, to serve

## METHOD

1. Preheat the oven to 140°C. Fill a kettle with water and boil. Arrange 4 small (½-cup capacity) ramekins in a large baking dish.

2. In a medium bowl, whisk the egg yolks and ¼ cup of the coconut sugar until pale and frothy. Add the coconut cream and whisk until smooth. Transfer mixture to a jug and pour into the prepared ramekins. Pour enough boiled water into the baking dish to reach halfway up the sides of the ramekins. Carefully transfer the dish to the oven and bake for 30–40 minutes, until the custard is just set.

3. Remove the ramekins from the baking dish and cool to room temperature. Sprinkle 1 teaspoon of the remaining coconut sugar over the surface of each custard. Caramelise using a blowtorch or by placing (very briefly) under a hot grill. Set aside for 5 minutes until the sugar hardens. Serve with fresh passionfruit.

Serves 4.

Don't Quit Sugar

# Blueberry Yogurt Semifreddo

'SEMIFREDDO' – ITALIAN FOR 'HALF COLD' – is a frozen dessert much like ice cream, but which doesn't require churning. It's traditionally made with whipped cream, though here I've substituted Greek yogurt to boost the protein content. The end result is tangy, light and wonderfully velvety. The recipe calls for raw egg yolks, so be sure to use the freshest eggs you can find.

## INGREDIENTS

300g frozen blueberries
5 large egg yolks
¼ cup raw honey
2 cups (500g) Greek yogurt

## METHOD

1. Line a 6-cup capacity loaf tin (21 x 11 x 6 cm) with plastic wrap.

2. Place the frozen blueberries in a small saucepan and, over medium-low heat, cook until the blueberries have softened and are beginning to break down. Set aside to cool to room temperature.

3. In a large bowl, use electric beaters or a stand mixer to beat the egg yolks and honey until thick and pale, about 5–8 minutes. Gently fold in the Greek yogurt. Add the blueberries (together with any syrup they've formed) and swirl to create a ripple effect. Pour the mixture into the prepared loaf tin and cover with plastic wrap. Freeze for 6 hours or overnight.

4. When ready to serve, remove the semifreddo from the freezer and allow it to soften at room temperature for 10–15 minutes. Invert it onto a large plate or cutting board, remove the plastic wrap and use a hot knife to slice thickly.

Don't Quit Sugar

# Frozen Strawberry Soufflés

THIS DESSERT IS A BIT OF A SHOWSTOPPER, perfect for impressing guests. It's essentially a honey-sweetened Italian meringue with the addition of fresh strawberries. Credit goes to my great-aunt, Gina, who's made a version of it every year at Passover for as long as I can remember.

## INGREDIENTS

½ cup raw honey
½ cup water
4 large egg whites
¼ tsp cream of tartar
750g (3 punnets) strawberries, hulled and finely chopped
juice of half a lemon

## METHOD

1. Choose six 1-cup capacity ramekins or teacups.

2. Cut six 30 x 15cm strips of baking paper. Fold each strip in half lengthways to create a 30 x 7.5cm rectangle. Wrap one strip around the top of each ramekin to create a collar and use tape to secure.

3. Combine the honey and water in a small saucepan. Bring to a boil over medium-high heat and continue to cook until the mixture reaches 121°C on a candy thermometer, about 15 minutes.

4. Meanwhile, in a stand mixer, whisk the egg whites and cream of tartar to soft peaks. With the motor running, pour the honey syrup into the egg whites in a steady stream. Add the strawberries and lemon juice and continue to beat the mixture at high speed until it is thick, glossy and pink.

5. Spoon into the prepared ramekins to a height 2–3cm above the rims and freeze overnight. Remove the paper collar and allow the 'soufflés' to soften at room temperature for 5 minutes before serving.

Serves 6.

If there's any mixture left over, simply freeze it in a container and eat it as you would a regular sorbet.

Basic candy thermometers don't cost more than a few dollars and are generally available from department stores and major supermarkets.

Don't Quit Sugar

# Honey-Roast Pears with Mascarpone

A TRULY DELECTABLE WINTER DESSERT. As the pears roast, their juices combine with the vanilla, honey and butter to form a heavenly pear-flavoured caramel. Mascarpone is a rich Italian cheese made from cream; if you're after something lighter, substitute Greek yogurt or fresh ricotta.

## INGREDIENTS

2 tbs unsalted butter

2 tbs raw honey

1 vanilla bean, halved lengthways and seeds scraped

4 ripe pears (Bosc work beautifully), peeled and halved

1 cup (250g) mascarpone

1 tsp ground cinnamon

## METHOD

1. Preheat the oven to 180°C.

2. In a small saucepan over medium-low heat, combine the butter, honey, half the vanilla seeds and 2 tablespoons of water. Stir until the butter has melted and the mixture is smooth.

3. Use a teaspoon or melon baller to neatly remove the seeds from each pear half. Arrange the pears, cut side up, in a medium baking dish (they should fit quite snugly). Drizzle with the honey–butter, cover with foil and bake for 20–25 minutes. Remove the foil, baste the pears with any baking juices and bake for an additional 10–15 minutes (uncovered), or until they are tender and caramelised. (The pears are ready when a small, sharp knife inserted into the thickest part meets no resistance.)

4. In a small bowl, stir together the mascarpone, cinnamon and remaining vanilla seeds.

5. Serve the pears – hot or cold – alongside the mascarpone.

Serves 4.

Don't Quit Sugar

# Nectarine and Raspberry Crumble

THIS IS ANOTHER DESSERT THAT COULD VERY EASILY DOUBLE AS BREAKFAST. Ensure you serve it with a big spoonful of Greek yogurt for protein (or eat it following a protein-heavy meal).

## INGREDIENTS

1kg ripe nectarines, halved and stones removed

300g fresh or frozen raspberries

2 cups rolled oats

¼ cup coconut sugar or rapadura sugar

½ tsp ground cinnamon

¼ tsp sea salt

100g butter or coconut oil, melted

## METHOD

1. Preheat the oven to 180°C and position a rack in the centre.

2. Slice the nectarine halves into 1cm wedges and tip them into a 25 x 30cm (or similar) baking dish. Scatter with the raspberries.

3. Using a food processor or high-speed blender, pulse 1 cup of the oats to a fine powder.

4. In a medium bowl, combine the processed oats, the remaining cup of rolled oats, the sugar, cinnamon and salt.

5. Drizzle in the butter or coconut oil and stir with a fork until the mixture is crumbly (almost the texture of wet sand).

6. Spread the crumble over the fruit and bake for 40–45 minutes, until the top is golden and the fruit is bubbling. Allow to cool for 15 minutes before serving.

---

If nectarines and raspberries aren't in season, feel free to substitute different fruits. Plums work beautifully, as do combinations of apple and blackberry, strawberry and rhubarb, or cherry and blueberry.

---

# Crustless Pumpkin Pie

THIS RECIPE MIMICS THE FLAVOURS OF THE NORTH AMERICAN CLASSIC but skips the (often difficult to make) pastry crust. The result is more of a pudding – smooth and custard-like in texture, with warm notes of cinnamon, ginger, allspice and cloves. Autumn in a bowl. I've substituted coconut milk for cream to make this dairy-free, but the recipe will also work with cream, whole milk, or a mixture of both.

## INGREDIENTS

butter or coconut oil, for greasing
3 cups mashed cooked pumpkin*
400ml can coconut milk
½ cup maple syrup
4 large eggs
1 tbs ground cinnamon
1 tsp ground nutmeg
1 tsp ground ginger
½ tsp ground cloves
½ tsp sea salt

## METHOD

1. Preheat the oven to 180°C and position a rack in the centre. Grease a 24cm round baking dish with butter or coconut oil.

2. Combine all ingredients in the bowl of a food processor and pulse until smooth. Alternatively, combine all ingredients in a large bowl and use electric beaters to beat until smooth. Pour the mixture into the prepared dish and tap it on a bench top to remove any air bubbles. Bake for 1 hour, or until a knife inserted in the centre withdraws clean. Cool to room temperature before serving.

*I find it easiest to simply roast halves of butternut pumpkin (drizzled with a little coconut oil) at 180°C until soft. Once cool enough to handle, scoop the flesh into a food processor (discard the skin and seeds) and pulse until smooth.

Don't Quit Sugar

# Dark Chocolate and Raspberry Truffles

TRUFFLES ARE TRADITIONALLY a combination of top-quality chocolate and heavy cream. This recipe substitutes Greek yogurt for a protein boost and delicious (though very subtle) tang. The hidden raspberries add sweetness and a beautiful burst of colour.

## INGREDIENTS

150g dark (70%) chocolate
½ cup Greek yogurt, cream or
  coconut cream
20 fresh raspberries
cocoa powder or dried shredded
  coconut for rolling, optional

## METHOD

1. Place chocolate in a heatproof bowl over a saucepan of simmering water (don't let the bowl touch the water). Use a metal spoon to stir occasionally, until the chocolate is melted and smooth. Remove the bowl from the heat and stir in the Greek yogurt, cream or coconut cream. Cover with plastic wrap and refrigerate until firm.

2. Working quickly, enclose a fresh raspberry in a heaped teaspoon of the chocolate mixture, then roll between your palms to form a ball shape. Repeat process for remaining berries. If desired, roll in cocoa powder or dried shredded coconut to coat. Place on a lined baking tray and refrigerate for an additional 30 minutes until set.

Makes 20.

# EXTRAS

# Grandma's Stewed Apples

DURING WINTER, WHEN THE VARIETY OF AVAILABLE FRUIT DWINDLES, I cook up big pots of stewed apples and pears to have on hand during the week. They're an incredibly versatile source of sucrose. Here are some ways to serve them:

- ❖ mix with yogurt and top with a sprinkling of coconut flakes
- ❖ use as a filling for a sweet omelette
- ❖ blend with milk and cinnamon for an 'apple pie' smoothie
- ❖ puree until smooth and combine with gelatin to form simple gummy squares
- ❖ serve alongside pâté, parmesan and crudités for a lunchtime ploughman's platter.

## INGREDIENTS

8 large Granny Smith apples
1 orange
1 lemon
½ cup water

## METHOD

1. Peel, core and dice the apples. Use a vegetable peeler to remove a 5cm strip of zest from both the orange and the lemon.

2. Combine the apples, zest, water and 1 tablespoon of lemon juice in a large saucepan. Cover with a lid and cook over medium-low heat, stirring occasionally, for 20–25 minutes, or until the apples have broken down.

3. Discard the orange and lemon zest and transfer the cooked apples to a glass jar or airtight container. Store in the refrigerator for up to 2 weeks.

Don't Quit Sugar

# Cherry Pie Oat Squares

A CROSS BETWEEN A MUESLI BAR, a crumble and a slice, these are a great lunchbox treat alongside your choice of protein: a couple of boiled eggs with crudités or a tub of Greek yogurt would each work wonderfully.

## INGREDIENTS

500g cherries, pitted (or thawed frozen cherries)
1 cinnamon stick
1 tsp finely grated orange zest
¼ cup orange juice

### For the dough

3 cups rolled oats
1 tsp cinnamon
1 tsp baking powder
½ tsp sea salt
1 cup stewed apples (recipe opposite) or store-bought jarred apple sauce
¼ cup raw honey
¼ cup water
1 tsp vanilla extract

## METHOD

1. Combine the cherries, cinnamon stick, orange zest and juice in a medium saucepan. Bring to a boil over medium-high heat; reduce the heat to low and simmer for 10 minutes, until the cherries have softened and released their juices. Use a slotted spoon to transfer the cherries to a heatproof bowl. Continue to simmer the orange-cherry liquid for an additional 5–10 minutes, until it has reduced and thickened slightly. Pour over the cherries and set aside to cool (discard the cinnamon stick).

2. Preheat the oven to 180°C. Line a 20cm square baking dish or cake tin with baking paper.

3. In a food processor or high-speed blender, pulse half the oats (1½ cups) to a fine powder. Tip them into a large bowl and add the remaining oats, cinnamon, baking powder and salt. Combine the stewed apples or apple sauce, honey, water and vanilla in a small bowl or jug and pour into the oat mixture. Mix thoroughly to form a sticky dough.

4. Spread half the dough into the base of the prepared baking dish, extending it to the edges and smoothing the top with the back of a spoon. Spoon over the cooled cherry mixture and then top with the remaining dough. Bake for 25–30 minutes, or until golden brown. Allow to cool before cutting into squares. Eat for breakfast or as a snack with a large spoonful of Greek yogurt.

# Frozen Yogurt-Covered Blueberries

THESE ARE A PERFECT ADDITION TO ANY FREEZER as an immediate fix for when blood sugar drops, or for any moment the munchies strike. Kids adore them, too.

### INGREDIENTS

200g Greek yogurt
1 tbs raw honey
1 cup frozen blueberries

### METHOD

1. Line a baking tray with baking paper.

2. In a shallow bowl, stir together the yogurt and honey. A handful at a time, toss the blueberries in the yogurt, ensuring they are coated. Remove with a toothpick and place on the prepared tray. Freeze for 1 hour, until the yogurt has frozen. Store in an airtight container in the freezer.

Don't Quit Sugar

# Smoothie How-to

THERE ARE SO MANY GOOD SMOOTHIE RECIPES and endless possible flavour combinations. I recommend experimenting with different fruits, liquids and add-ins and discovering which ingredients work best for you.

One important guideline
Ensure your smoothies always contain a balance of natural sugar, protein and fat to balance blood sugar, reduce stress and increase satiety.

Natural sugars
Whole seasonal fruit, orange juice, pitted medjool dates, cooled stewed apples, cooled cooked pumpkin or sweet potato (excellent with cinnamon and milk), raw honey or maple syrup, coconut water, rolled oats (preferably soaked in water overnight to improve digestibility)

Proteins
Whole cow's or goat's milk, Greek yogurt, gelatin, whole raw eggs (ensure they're organic, free-range and very fresh)

Fats
Whole cow's or goat's milk, Greek yogurt, coconut milk, dried shredded or desiccated coconut, coconut oil, cream, raw egg yolks (again, ensure they're organic, free-range and very fresh)

Add-ins
Cocoa powder, ground cinnamon, fresh mint leaves, vanilla extract or scraped vanilla seeds (from a whole vanilla bean), a shot of espresso

For the following recipes, simply combine all ingredients in a blender and blend until smooth. Each recipe makes one smoothie but can easily be doubled or tripled.

## Strawberry-Mango

1 cup fresh strawberries, halved
½ cup frozen mango, chopped
1 cup (250g) Greek yogurt
½ cup coconut water
1 tsp raw honey, optional

## Orange Creamsicle

1 cup whole cow's or goat's milk
1 cup freshly squeezed orange juice
1 frozen banana
1 raw egg
1 tsp coconut oil

## Cocoa-Raspberry Coconut Milk

½ cup canned coconut milk
1 cup water
1 cup frozen raspberries
2 medjool dates, pitted
1 tbs cocoa powder
2 tbs Great Lakes gelatin

# Perfect Hot Chocolate

A COMBINATION OF MILK, NATURAL SUGAR AND SALT before bed will help to lower stress hormones, balance blood sugar, increase body temperature, improve circulation and support metabolism – everything necessary for a sound night's sleep.

## INGREDIENTS

¼ cup cocoa powder

3 cups whole milk

2 tbs raw honey, or more to taste

1 vanilla bean, halved lengthways and seeds scraped, or 1 tsp vanilla extract

½ tsp ground cinnamon

½ tsp sea salt

## METHOD

In a small saucepan, whisk the cocoa powder, ½ cup milk and honey until smooth. Add the remaining milk, vanilla seeds, empty vanilla bean, cinnamon and salt. Stir over medium-low heat until scalding (small bubbles should form around the edge of the pan). Divide between mugs.

Makes 3 cups.

Cocoa contains a stimulant – theobromine – which can produce anxiety, restlessness or insomnia in sensitive people. If you find that it affects you, skip the hot chocolate and opt for a mug of cinnamon-spiced, honey-sweetened warm milk instead.

Don't Quit Sugar

# Basic Beef Broth

BONE BROTH IS A MICRONUTRIENT-RICH INFUSION made by simmering gelatinous animal bones with vegetables and herbs. It is high in calcium, magnesium and the anti-inflammatory amino acids proline and glycine. These reduce stress; heal and maintain the integrity of the intestinal lining; promote detoxification and immune function; and support collagen biosynthesis for the health of bones, teeth, nails and skin.

There is simply no comparison to store-bought stock or broth varieties, the vast majority of which lack gelatin and contain additives or MSG.

In making your broth, ensure you source high-quality bones from grass-fed cattle or pasture-raised chickens. You'll be extracting and concentrating the micronutrients in the bones, so you want the animal to have been as healthy as possible.

## INGREDIENTS

2–2.5kg beef bones (include some marrow bones, if you can get any)
2 tbs vinegar
2 large carrots, halved
2 large celery stalks, halved
1 medium brown onion, quartered (you can leave the skin on)
1 head of garlic, halved horizontally
2 bay leaves
1 tsp whole black peppercorns

---

To make a chicken broth, simply replace the beef bones with chicken carcasses and feet (if you can get them). Don't worry about the initial roasting; just place the carcasses straight into your pot, add the vinegar and cover with water.

## METHOD

1. Preheat the oven to 180°C. Arrange the bones in a large roasting tray and bake for 20–30 minutes, until browned. (This step isn't mandatory, but it will impart a deeper flavour to the finished broth.)

2. Tip the bones into your largest pot and add the vinegar. Fill the pot with water, ensuring that all the bones are submerged, and then let it sit at room temperature for 20–30 minutes. During this time, the vinegar will help to leach the minerals (particularly calcium) out of the bones.

3. Add the vegetables, garlic, bay leaves and peppercorns to the pot, place over high heat and bring to a boil. Use a spoon to skim any froth or scum that rises to the surface.

4. Reduce the heat to low and simmer for 4–6 hours. Allow to cool slightly and then strain into a large bowl, discarding the bones and vegetables.

5. Refrigerate overnight, or until the fat has solidified on the surface. Use a spoon or your hands to remove the fat (it usually comes off quite easily in shards) and then divide the broth between glass jars or containers. Freeze it for up to 3 months or refrigerate for up to 1 week.

# Tips for Eating Out

Indulging in a café breakfast?
Good choices include:

- Poached eggs on buttered sourdough.
- A cheesy omelette (cooked in butter) and a tall glass of OJ.
- Seasonal fruit with yogurt or ricotta.
- Bircher-style muesli with fruit and yogurt.
- Porridge with compote, plus milk or cream.
- Baked Moroccan-style eggs with sourdough for dipping.

Forgot to pack your own work lunch?
Opt to buy:

- A sourdough sandwich with roast beef or sliced hard-boiled eggs, and salad. A piece of fruit to finish.
- Sushi rolls with raw or cooked tuna and prawns.
- A Thai- or Vietnamese-style rice noodle soup with seafood or thinly sliced beef and pineapple.
- A store-bought salad with roast root vegetables and your choice of protein (though watch out for canola-based dressings and mayonnaises, which are high in polyunsaturated fatty acids).

Dining out for dinner?

- Keep it simple with grilled protein (steak, chicken or fish) and root vegetables or a baked potato.
- For something light, a cheese and roasted root vegetable salad is great – think pumpkin and feta or beetroot and goat's cheese. Just ask for a dressing with extra virgin olive oil.
- If you're dining Asian-style, opt for coconut-based curries with rice or rice noodles, fragrant salads with grilled beef or chicken, or a steamed whole fish with greens and rice. Stir-fried dishes are usually vegetable-oil (and therefore PUFA) heavy.
- Desserts can certainly be indulged in: gelato, panna cotta, crème brûlée, chocolate mousse or poached fruit and custard typically contain only pure, nourishing ingredients.

Stuck for portable snack ideas? Easy.

- A piece of ripe seasonal fruit with your choice of protein – a tub of yogurt, a hard-boiled egg or a chunk of quality parmesan cheese.
- Medjool dates stuffed with ricotta or feta.
- A homemade smoothie (simply store it in a glass jar).
- A few squares of quality dark (70%) chocolate – perfect for balancing blood sugar between meals.

Don't Quit Sugar

# 7-DAY MEAL PLANNER

| Day | Breakfast | Snack | Lunch |
|-----|-----------|-------|-------|
| 1 | Puffed blueberry omelette (page 60) | Homemade smoothie (page 143) | Prawn, watermelon and feta salad (page 81) |
| 2 | Banana split in a jar (page 71) | Wedge of sweet potato tortilla (page 55) | Sourdough sandwich with salad and your choice of protein; piece of fruit |
| 3 | Pumpkin baked eggs (page 67) | Grandma's stewed apples with fresh ricotta or Greek yogurt (page 140) | Roasted beetroot with orange zest and labneh (page 77) |
| 4 | Warm maple-apple bircher (page 68) | Seasonal fruit and a chunk of parmesan | Spring vegetable casserole with eggs (page 90) |
| 5 | Little baked ricotta cakes with plums (page 52) | Seasonal fruit and 1–2 hard-boiled eggs | Thai- or Vietnamese-style rice noodle soup with seafood |
| 6 | Two-tone coconut jelly with mango (page 56) | Homemade smoothie (page 143) | Seared beef fillet with figs, parmesan and rocket (page 74) |
| 7 | Mexican egg skillet with sourdough (page 63) | Yogurt-covered blueberries (page 142) | Grilled haloumi with fresh cherries and basil (page 93) |

Don't Quit Sugar

| Snack | Dinner | Dessert (optional) |
|---|---|---|
| Baked apple chips with fresh ricotta or Greek yogurt (page 68) | Mexican mince-stuffed sweet potatoes (page 106) | Seasonal fruit |
| A few squares of quality dark chocolate | Spinach and ricotta gnocchi with pumpkin sauce and roast tomatoes (page 112) | Honey-roast pears with mascarpone (page 130) |
| Seasonal fruit and a mug of homemade bone broth (page 145) | Spiced chicken with apricots and olives (page 108) | Perfect hot chocolate (page 144) |
| Yogurt-covered blueberries (page 142) | Vietnamese grilled chicken with lychee salad (page 102) | Dark chocolate and raspberry truffles (page 137) |
| A few squares of quality dark chocolate | Lamb shank tagine with dates and prunes (page 98) | Greek yogurt with berries |
| Medjool dates stuffed with ricotta or feta | Simple baked fish and root vegetables (page 105) | Blueberry yogurt semifreddo (page 126) |
| Banana split in a jar (page 71) | Your choice of protein with salad and a baked potato | Seasonal fruit |

# Further Reading

## INTERESTING STUDIES AND JOURNAL ARTICLES

Adolph M, Eckart A, Eckart J. Fructose vs. glucose in total parenteral nutrition in critically ill patients. Anaesthesist. 1995 Nov;44(11):770-81.

Ahmed Z, Khan MS, Khan MA, ul Haq A, Rahman J. Seminal fructose in various classes of infertile patients. Pak J Physiol 2010;6(1):36-8.

Al-Waili NS. Natural honey lowers plasma glucose, C-reactive protein, homocysteine, and blood lipids in healthy, diabetic, and hyperlipidemic subjects: comparison with dextrose and sucrose. J Med Food. 2004 Spring;7(1):100-7.

Anundi I, King J, Owen DA, Schneider H, Lemasters JJ, Thurman RG. Fructose prevents hypoxic cell death in liver. Am J Physiol. 1987 Sep;253(3 Pt 1):G390-6.

Buchman AL, Ament ME, Sohel M, et al. Choline deficiency causes reversible hepatic abnormalities in patients receiving parenteral nutrition: proof of a human choline requirement: a placebo-controlled trial. J Parenter Enteral Nutr. Sep-Oct 2001;25(5):260-268.

Chong MF, Fielding BA, Frayn KN. Mechanisms for the acute effect of fructose on postprandial lipemia. Am J Clin Nutr. 2007;85:1511–20.

Coelho RC, Hermsdorff HH, Bressan J. Anti-inflammatory properties of orange juice: possible favorable molecular and metabolic effects. Plant Foods Hum Nutr. 2013 Mar;68(1):1-10.

Cozma AI, Sievenpiper JL, De Souza RJ, Chiavaroli L, Ha V, Wang DD, Mirrahimi A et al. Effect of fructose on glycemic control in diabetes: a systematic review and meta-analysis of controlled feeding trials. Diabetes Care 2012;35(7):1611–20.

Dolan LC, Potter SM, Burdock GA. Evidence-based review on the effect of normal dietary consumption of fructose on development of hyperlipidemia and obesity in healthy, normal weight individuals. Crit Rev Food Sci Nutr. 2010 Jan;50(1):53-84.

Dolan LC, Potter SM, Burdock GA. Evidence-based review on the effect of normal dietary consumption of fructose on blood lipids and body weight of overweight and obese individuals. Crit Rev Food Sci Nutr. 2010 Nov;50(10):889-918.

Ghanim H, Mohanty P, Pathak R, Chaudhuri A, Sia CL, Dandona P. Orange juice or fructose intake does not induce oxidative and inflammatory response. Diabetes Care. 2007 Jun;30(6):1406-11.

Ghanim H, Sia CL, Upadhyay M, Korzeniewski K, Viswanathan P, Abuaysheh S, Mohanty P, Dandona P. Orange juice neutralizes the proinflammatory effect of a high-fat, high-carbohydrate meal and prevents endotoxin increase and Toll-like receptor expression. Am J Clin Nutr. 2010 Apr;91(4):940-9.

Gribel NV, Pashinski VG. The antitumor properties of honey. Vopr Onkol. 1990;36(6):704-9.

Hawkins M, Gabriely I, Wozniak R, Vilcu C, Shamoon H, Rossetti L. Fructose improves the ability of hyperglycemia per se to regulate glucose production in type 2 diabetes. Diabetes. 2002 Mar;51(3):606-14.

Hellerstein MK, Christiansen M, Kaempfer S, et al. Measurement of de novo lipogenesis in humans using stable isotopes. J Clin Invest 1991;87:1841-52.

Hendler RG, Walesky M, Sherwin RS. Sucrose substitution in prevention and reversal of the fall in metabolic rate accompanying hypocaloric diets. Am J Med. 1986 Aug;81(2):280-4.

Hill JO, Prentice AM. Sugar and body weight regulation. Am J Clin Nutr. 1995 Jul;62(1 Suppl): 264S-273S.

Holt SH, Miller JC, Petocz P. An insulin index of foods: the insulin demand generated by 1000-kJ

Don't Quit Sugar

portions of common foods. Am J Clin Nutr. 1997 Nov;66(5):1264-76.

Hue L, Taegtmeyer H. The Randle cycle revisited: a new head for an old hat. Am J Physiol Endocrinol Metab. 2009 Sep;297(3):E578-91.

Jauniaux E, Hempstock J, Teng C, Battaglia FC, Burton GJ. Polyol concentrations in the fluid compartments of the human conceptus during the first trimester of pregnancy: maintenance of redox potential in a low oxygen environment. J Clin Endocrinol Metab. 2005 Feb;90(2):1171-5.

Kim J, Song G, Wu G, Bazer FW. Functional roles of fructose. Proc Natl Acad Sci USA. 2012 Jun 19;109(25):E1619-28.

Lindeberg S, Berntorp E, Nilsson-Ehle P, Terént A, Vessby B. Age relations of cardiovascular risk factors in a traditional Melanesian society: the Kitava Study. Am J Clin Nutr. 1997 Oct;66(4):845-52.

Lindeberg S, Eliasson M, Lindahl B, Ahrén B. Low serum insulin in traditional Pacific Islanders: the Kitava Study. Metabolism. 1999 Oct;48(10): 1216-19.

Livesy G. Fructose ingestion: dose-dependent responses in health research. J Nutr. 2009 Jun;139(6):1246S-1252S.

Lowndes J, Kawiecki D, Angelopoulos T, Rippe J. Fructose containing sugars do not result in an atherogenic lipid profile when consumed as part of a eucaloric (weight-stable) diet. Circulation. 2010;122:A10906.

Lowndes J, Kawiecki D, Angelopoulos T, Rippe J. Fructose containing sugars do not cause changes in weight, body composition or abdominal fat when consumed as part of a eucaloric (weight-stable) diet. Obesity. 2010;18: Suppl 2:S51.

Lowndes J, Kawiecki D, Pardo S, Nguyen V, Melanson KJ, Yu Z, Rippe JM. The effects of four hypocaloric diets containing different levels of sucrose or high fructose corn syrup on weight loss and related parameters. Nutr J. 2012 Aug 6;11:55.

Lowndes J, Sinnett S, Yu Z, Rippe J. Effects of fructose containing sugars on lipids, blood pressure and uric acid when consumed at up to 90th percentile population consumption levels. Circulation. 2012;126:A13066.

Marlowe FW, Berbesque JC. Tubers as fallback foods and their impact on Hadza hunter-gatherers. Am J Phys Anthropol. 2009 Dec;140(4):751-8.

McDevitt R, Bott SJ, Harding M. De novo lipogenesis during controlled overfeeding with sucrose or glucose in lean and obese women. Am J Clin Nutr. 2001;74:737-746.

McGuinness OP, Cherrington AD. Effects of fructose on hepatic glucose metabolism. Curr Opin Clin Nutr Metab Care 2003;6(4):441–8.

Meyer BJ, van der Merwe M, Du Plessis DG, de Bruin EJ, Meyer AC. Some physiological effects of a mainly fruit diet in man. S Afr Med J. 1971 Feb 20;45(8):191-5.

Moran TH. Fructose and satiety. J Nutr. 2009 Jun;139(6):1253S-1256S.

Osei K, Bossetti B. Dietary fructose as a natural sweetener in poorly controlled type 2 diabetes: a 12-month crossover study of effects on glucose, lipoprotein and apolipoprotein metabolism. Diabet Med 1989;6:506–11.

Randle PJ, Garland PB, Hales CN, Newsholme EA. The glucose fatty-acid cycle. Its role in insulin sensitivity and the metabolic disturbances of diabetes mellitus. Lancet 1963;1:785–9.

Rippe JM, Angelopoulos TJ. Sucrose, high-fructose corn syrup and fructose, their metabolism and potential health effects: what do we really know? Adv Nutr. 2013;4:236-245.

Rodríguez MC, Parra MD, Marques-Lopes I, De Morentin BE, González A, Martínez JA. Effects of two energy-restricted diets containing different fruit amounts on body weight loss and macronutrient oxidation. Plant Foods Hum Nutr. 2005 Dec;60(4):219-24.

Sievenpiper JL, de Souza RJ, Mirrahimi A, Yu ME, Carleton AJ, Beyene J, Chiavaroli L, Di Buono M, Jenkins AL, Leiter LA, Wolever TM, Kendall CW, Jenkins DJ. Effect of fructose on body weight in controlled feeding trials: a systematic review and meta-analysis. Ann Intern Med. 2012 Feb 21;156(4):291-304.

Simonson DC, Tappy L, Jequier E, Felber JP, DeFronzo RA. Normalization of carbohydrate-induced thermogenesis by fructose in insulin-resistant states. Am J Physiol 1988; 254: E201–7.

Sinnett PF, Whyte HM. Epidemiological studies in a total highland population, Tukisenta, New Guinea. Cardiovascular disease and relevant clinical, electrocardiographic, radiological and biochemical findings. J Chronic Dis. 1973 May;26(5):265-90.

Spasojevi I, Baji A, Jovanovi K, Spasi M, Andjus P. Protective role of fructose in the metabolism of astroglial C6 cells exposed to hydrogen peroxide. Carbohydr Res. 2009 Sep 8;344(13):1676-81.

Sun SZ, Empie MW. Fructose metabolism in humans – what isotopic tracer studies tell us. Nutrition & Metabolism 2012;9:89.

Tappy L, Jéquier E. Fructose and dietary thermogenesis. Am J Clin Nutr. 1993 Nov;58(5 Suppl):766S-770S.

Watford M. Small amounts of dietary fructose dramatically increase hepatic glucose uptake through a novel mechanism of glucokinase activation. Nutr Rev 2002;60(8):253–7.

White JS. Challenging the fructose hypothesis: new perspectives on fructose consumption and metabolism. Adv Nutr 2013;4:246-256.

Zeisel SH, da Costa N. Choline: an essential nutrient for public health. Nutr Rev. 2009 November;67(11):615–623.

## BOOKS WORTH READING

Barnes BO, Barnes CW. Hope for hypoglycaemia: it's not your mind, it's your liver. Fries Communications; 1989.

Barnes BO. Hypothyroidism: the unsuspected illness. Toronto: Fitzhenry & Whiteside Ltd; 1976.

Guyton A, Hall J. Textbook of Medical Physiology. 11th ed. Saunders; 2006.

Lindeberg S. Food and Western disease: Health and nutrition from an evolutionary perspective. Wiley-Blackwell; 2010.

Ling GN. Revolution in the physiology of the living cell. Krieger Pub Co; 1991.

Ling GN. Life at the cell and below-cell level: the hidden history of a fundamental revolution in biology. Pacific Investment Research Inc; 2001.

Martin CR. Endocrine physiology. Oxford University Press; 1985.

Peat R. Nutrition for women; 1993.

Selye H. Stress in health and disease. Butterworth-Heinemann Ltd; 1976.

Selye H. The stress of life. McGraw Hill; 1978.

## WEBSITES AND BLOGS TO EXPAND YOUR KNOWLEDGE

http://raypeat.com/articles/

http://dannyroddy.com/

http://www.andrewkimblog.com/

http://www.functionalps.com/

http://nutritionbynature.com.au/

http://www.thenutritioncoach.com.au/blog/

Don't Quit Sugar

# Index

**A**
adrenaline  10
ageing  13
AGEs (Advanced Glycation End products)  21–22
amino acids  49
amylin  18
anabolic  44
animal products
    in evolutionary diet  16
    for protein  49
anti-nutrients  32
antioxidants  22
apples
    chips  68
    Grandma's stewed  140
    warm maple–apple bircher  68
apricots, spiced chicken with  108
artificial sweetener  35
Atkins diet  19


**B**
banana split in jar  71
bedtime snack  40
beef
    basic broth  145
    Mexican mince-stuffed sweet potatoes  102
    open-face steak sandwich with quick beetroot relish  111
    seared fillet with figs, parmesan and rocket  74
beetroot  29
    relish  111
    roasted with orange zest and labneh  77
biofeedback  43
bircher, warm maple–apple  68
blood sugar balance

achieving  36–37
fructose for  41
signs of low blood sugar  39
blueberries
    blueberry omelette, puffed  60
    blueberry yogurt semifreddo  126
    frozen yogurt-covered  142
body fat gain from sugar  16–18, 19
body heat production  17, 20
body mass index (BMI)  17
body temperature  43, 45
body weight loss  41, 45
bone broth  49, 145
breakfast  38, 51
bromelain  82
broth, beef or chicken  145
brown sugar  34
butter  49


**C**
calcium  40
candida  22–23
candy thermometers  129
cane sugar  34
carbohydrates, complex  20, 26
carbon dioxide ($CO_2$)  22
carrots  29
    carrot cake pancakes, flour-free  59
casserole, spring vegetable with eggs  90
caster sugar  34
catabolic  44
cell function  18–19
ceviche, snapper, with mango and coconut  85
cheesecake, mango and passionfruit ricotta  119
cherries
    cherry pie oat squares  141

grilled haloumi with  93
chicken
   chicken broth  145
   coconut curry soup with rice noodles and
     eggs  115
   and rice dumpling soup  89
   spiced, with apricots and olives  108
   Vietnamese grilled, with lychee salad  102
chips
   apple  68
   sweet potato  85
chocolate
   chocolate cake  120
   chocolate mousse  123
   chocolate sauce  71
   hot  144
   and raspberry truffles  137
chocolate, dark  123
choline deficiency  21
chronic energy surplus  17
cocoa  144
  cocoa-raspberry coconut milk smoothie  143
coconut
   coconut crème brûlée  124
   coconut curry soup with rice noodles and
     eggs  115
   coconut jelly with mango  56
   snapper ceviche with mango and  85
coconut milk  49
  cocoa-raspberry coconut milk smoothie  143
coconut oil  20, 49
coconut palm sugar  34
coconut water  56
coffee  38
collagen  49
complex carbohydrates  20, 26
controlled studies  17
corn syrup  35
cortisol  10, 38
cream  49
crème brûlée, coconut  124
crumble
   cherry pie oat squares  141
   nectarine and raspberry  133

**D**
dairy  31, 49
dates  33
   chocolate cake  120
   lamb shank tagine with  98
de novo lipogenesis (DNL)  17, 19
defensive substances  32
desiccated coconut  49
diabetes
   advantages of fructose  20
   AGEs and  22
   myth of sugar as cause of  18–19
   Type 2  12
digestive system  11, 26
disaccharides  25–26
DNL (de novo lipogenesis)  17, 19
dressing
   orange zest  77
   pomegranate molasses  97
   pumpkin puree  112
   spiced chicken marinade  108
dried coconut flesh  49
dry goods staples  47
dumplings, chicken and rice  89

**E**
eating out tips  146
egg yolks  21
eggs  38, 49, 123
   coconut crème brûlée  124
   coconut curry soup with rice noodles and
     115
   Mexican egg skillet  63
   puffed blueberry omelette  60
   pumpkin baked  67
   spring vegetable casserole with  90
eggplant, fig and mozzarella sandwiches  86
endotoxin  21
epigenetic adaptation to grain consumption
  32
ethnicity and lactase production  31
exclusionary eating  7, 45
exercise  44

Don't Quit Sugar

**F**
fats
    blood sugar and  36
    in evolutionary diet  16
    fresh produce staples  49
    metabolism of  13, 19
    Randle cycle  19
    as source of cellular energy  9
    sugar conversion to  17
fatty acids *see* polyunsaturated fatty acids
fatty liver *see* non-alcoholic fatty liver disease
feta, prawn and watermelon salad  81
fight or flight stress hormones  10
figs
    eggplant, fig and mozzarella sandwiches  86
    seared beef fillet with  74
fire  15
fish  49
    barbecued whole snapper with papaya salsa  101
    chilli lime tuna skewers with shaved pineapple  82
    simple baked, and root vegetables  105
    snapper ceviche with mango and coconut  85
flaked coconut  49
flour substitute  47
fluids  39
foetal development  41–42
fructose  19
    for blood sugar balance  41
    for body weight loss  41
    choline deficiency  21
    conversion to fat in liver  19–20
    foetal development and  41–42
    insulin release and  26
    as monosaccharide  25–26
    non-alcoholic fatty liver disease  21
    recommended intake  41
    in treatment of insulin resistance and diabetes  20
fruit
    anti-stress minerals  40
    benefits of  28
    in evolutionary diet  15
    fresh produce staples  48
    sugars in  26
    wild varieties  16

**G**
galactose  25
gelatin  49
genetic adaptation to grain consumption  32
GLP-1  18
gluconeogenesis  10, 20
glucose  9, 20
    insulin release and  26
    metabolism of  12
    as monosaccharide  25–26
glutathione  22
gluten intolerance  68
glycaemic control  20
glycation  21–22
glycogen  10, 17
gnocchi, spinach and ricotta  112
goat's cheese, baked ratatouille with  78
grains  20, 26
    anti-nutrients in  32
    preparation of  32
granulated cane sugar  34
Great Lakes beef gelatin powder  49

**H**
haloumi, grilled, with fresh cherries and basil  93
heart rate  43
hepatic glucokinase  20
HFCS (high fructose corn syrup)  35
high blood sugar  18
high fructose corn syrup (HFCS)  35
honey  15, 33
honey butter  130
hot chocolate  144
human evolutionary diet  15–16

**I**

icing sugar  34
immune system  11, 22–23
immunoglobulin A (IgA)  22–23
increased satiety  18
insomnia  13, 40
insulin  18
insulin release  26, 36
insulin resistance  12, 18, 19, 20, 41
insulin sensitivity  18
intestinal health  11
Inuit  16


**J**

jelly, coconut, with mango  56


**L**

labneh  77
lactase enzyme  31
lactate  19
lactose  31
lactose intolerance  31
lamb
    lamb shank tagine with dates and prunes
      98
    slow-roast shoulder with pomegranate
      molasses and Turkish spoon salad  97
legumes  20, 26
leptin  18
lipolysis  10
liquids and condiments staples  47
liver  12, 19, 37
    achieving sugar storage in  39
    foetal development and  42
    as food source  21
    non-alcoholic fatty liver disease  19, 21
low blood sugar signs  39
low-carbohydrate diets  19
low-sugar diets  19
lychee salad  102

**M**

Maasai of Africa  16
mango
    coconut jelly with  56
    and passionfruit ricotta cheesecake  119
    snapper ceviche with coconut and  85
    strawberry-mango smoothie  143
maple syrup, pure, Grade B  34
maple–apple bircher, warm  68
marinade: spiced chicken  108
mascarpone, honey-roast pears with  130
meat on bone  49
meat sources  49
medjool dates *see* dates
melatonin  40
melon
    with passionfruit syrup and whipped ricotta
      64
    watermelon, prawn and feta salad  81
metabolism
    body temperature and  43, 45
    effects of quitting sugar on  10–11
    signs of disorder in  13
Mexican egg skillet  63
Mexican mince-stuffed sweet potatoes  106
mice versus human studies  19
milk  49
milk cheeses  49
milk sugar  31
milk with honey  40
mocha mousse  123
molasses  34
monosaccharides  25–26
mousse, mocha  123
mozzarella in carrozza  86
muesli: warm maple–apple bircher  68


**N**

nectarine and raspberry crumble  133
non-alcoholic fatty liver disease  19, 21
nut oils  49

Don't Quit Sugar

**O**

oat square dough  141
obesity *see* body fat gain from sugar
oestrogen  12
oil types  49
olive oil  49
olives, spiced chicken with  108
omelette, puffed blueberry  60
orange creamsicle smoothie  143
orange juice  30
orange zest dressing  77


**P**

Paleo diet  16, 19
palm sugar  34
pancakes, flour-free carrot cake  59
pancreas  12, 26
pantry staples  47–49
papaya salsa  101
passionfruit
    mango and passionfruit ricotta cheesecake
      119
    syrup  64
peaches  26
pears, honey-roast, with mascarpone  130
pectin  28
pie
    cherry pie oat squares  141
    crustless pumpkin  134
pineapple salad, shaved  82
placental development  41–42
plums, ricotta cakes baked with  52
polysaccharides  26
polyunsaturated fatty acids (PUFA)  12,
    18–19, 22, 41, 49
pomegranate molasses dressing  97
potatoes  20, 26, 29
prawn, watermelon and feta salad  81
primate diet  15
processed foods  35
progesterone  12
protein
    in AGEs  21–22
    balanced with sugars  18, 40
    blood sugar and  36
    in evolutionary diet  16
    fresh produce staples  49
prunes, lamb shank tagine with  98
PUFA (polyunsaturated fatty acids)  12,
    18–19, 22, 41, 49
pumpkin
    pie, crustless  134
    pumpkin baked eggs  67
    puree  112
puree, pumpkin  112
pyruvate dehydrogenase  20


**R**

Randle cycle  19
raspberries
    cocoa-raspberry coconut milk smoothie
      143
    dark chocolate and raspberry truffles  137
    raspberry and nectarine crumble  133
ratatouille, baked, with goat's cheese  78
raw sugar  34
reduced appetite suppression  19
regular meals  39
relish, beetroot  111
reproductive system  12, 41–42
resting energy expenditure  18
restrictive eating  7, 45
rice: chicken and rice dumpling soup  89
rice noodles  115
rice syrup  35
ricotta
    mango and passionfruit ricotta cheesecake
      119
    ricotta cakes, baked, with plums  52
    spinach and ricotta gnocchi  112
    whipped  64
rolled oats ground  47
root vegetables *see* starchy root vegetables

**S**

salads
    lychee  102
    prawn, watermelon and feta  81
    Turkish spoon salad  97
salsa, papaya  101
salt  38
sandwiches
    eggplant, fig and mozzarella  86
    steak, open-face, with quick beetroot relish
        111
seed oils  49
selenium  81
semen  41
semifreddo, blueberry yogurt  126
serotonin  40
seven-day meal planner  147
sex drive hormones  12
sexual appetite  12
shakshuka  63
shellfish  49, 81
shredded coconut  49
sleeping  13, 40
smoothies  143
snapper
    barbecued whole with papaya salsa  101
    ceviche with mango and coconut  85
soft drinks  35
soufflés, frozen strawberry  129
soup
    chicken and rice dumpling  89
    coconut curry, with rice noodles and eggs
        115
spices and herbs staples  47–48
spinach and ricotta gnocchi  112
split, banana, in jar  71
spring vegetable casserole with eggs  90
staples for pantry  47–49
starch
    blood sugar balance  36–37
    glucose molecules in  26
    sources of  47
starchy root vegetables
    benefits of  26, 29

in evolutionary diet  15–16
    fresh produce staples  48
stevia  35
strawberries
    crushed  71
    frozen strawberry soufflés  129
    strawberry-mango smoothie  143
stress in exercise  44
stress response system  10–13
sucrose  20, 25–26
sugar
    best sources of  26–34
    blood sugar balance  36–37
    dangers of quitting  9–14
    disaccharides see lactose; sucrose
    in human evolution  15–16
    metabolism of  19
    monosaccharides see fructose; galactose;
        glucose
    polysaccharides see starch
    recommended intake  37
    as source of cellular energy  7, 9
    stress response system and  10–13
sugar alternatives  35
sugar cravings  37
supplementation  47
sweating  13
sweet potato  16, 29
    chips  85
    Mexican mince-stuffed  102
    tortilla  55


**T**

tagine, lamb shank, with dates and prunes  98
testosterone  12
Thai coconuts  56
theobromine  144
thermogenesis  17, 20
thymus gland  11
thyroid function  21
thyroid gland  10
thyroid hormones T3 and T4  10–11, 17, 39,
    81

Don't Quit Sugar

tinned food staples  48
tomatoes
   roast  112
   tomato-baked eggs  63
tortilla, sweet potato  55
toxins  32
truffles, dark chocolate and raspberry  137
tuna skewers, chilli lime, with shaved
  pineapple  82
turbinado sugar  34
Turkish spoon salad  97
Type 2 diabetes  12
   advantages of fructose  20
   AGEs and  22
   myth of sugar as cause of  18–19


**U**
United States sugar consumption  35
urination  13


**V**
vegetable oils  49
vegetable recipes

fresh produce staples  48
  lychee salad  102
  ratatouille, baked, with goats cheese  78
  simple baked fish and root vegetables  105
  spring vegetable casserole with eggs  90
vegetables *see* starchy root vegetables
Vietnamese grilled chicken with lychee salad
  102
visceral fat  19


**W**
watermelon, prawn and feta salad  81
weight gain *see* body fat gain from sugar
weight loss *see* body weight loss
white sugar  34
whole grains *see* grains


**Y**
yogurt
   blueberry yogurt semifreddo  126
   frozen yogurt-covered blueberries  142
   yogurt cheese (labneh)  77